INSIDE LOOKING IN

INSIDE
LOOKING IN

a Memoir by Mister Overstreet

Lyric
Literature
Publishing

I dedicate this book to my daughter, Genesis Lyric. You are the reason I Never gave up and witnessed this journey first-hand. I hope this inspires you to Achieve whatever you set your mind to.
God got your back and so do I.
I love you.

Dad

Acknowledgements

First and foremost, I Thank and Praise God.

To my wife, Queen. You've been very supportive, patient, and encouraging during this entire process. I love you immensely for that and much more. To Areion and Jasi, thank you for being such wonderful additions to my Life. You both are rock stars! I love you and I'm here for you always, know that!

I'd like to thank my wonderful parents, Craig and Gloria Robinson. I couldn't have asked for better living examples. My upbringing has shaped my giving character and never quit attitude. Thank you for raising me, Kenya, and Rico with so much love and laying a foundation of Faith that has saved my Life countless times. I love you both very much!

Mama Nita...thank you for always supporting my love for Hip Hop music. You bought me my first 2 cassette tapes from LL Cool J and De La Soul, Thank you!

A special shout out goes out to the man who introduced me to Hip Hop music, my Uncle Lonzo! Look what playing "Double Dutch Bus" did for me! I'm eternally grateful.

To my siblings Rico, Kenya, Nicky, Tammy, Teka, Tory, Channesia, and Chris...my day one supporters! Thanks for always rooting for ya brother! I love you all!

There are 3 individuals who Refused to let me do this project on my own and challenged me constantly to stay the course. A HUGE Thank you to Jerrold Daniels, Ydrate Nelson, and Areshia McFarlin. You all sacrificed Hours of your time and talent to make this possible, Thank YOU!

To the Hip Hop group that has heavily influenced and inspired my life and dominated my music playlist for years, A Tribe Called Quest, thank you! Long live Phife Dawg!

Lastly, I'd like to acknowledge every single one of YOU who had a hand in supporting me along this journey. I don't want to get caught up in name dropping every single person, because that would take an eternity due to the large amount of family, friends, and supporters that I am so blessed to have in my life, most of whom have been mentioned in this book and others to follow in this series. I appreciate every Word of encouragement, every Push, every Prayer, every Cheer, every Phone call, every Conversation, every Cosign, every Beat, every Mix, every Ride, every Vote, and every Dollar! None of this is possible without your support, Thank YOU!

Contents

1. Start it Up   1

2. 8 Million Stories   3

3. Can I Kick It   13

4. Motivators   24

5. Pad & Pen   28

6. Stressed Out   33

7. Lost Somebody   38

8. Bugging Out   43

9. The Love   53

10. Mr. Muhammad   57

11. Excursions   62

12. Find a Way   68

13. Lyrics to Go   75

14. Check the Rhime   80

15. What?!   89

16. We Can Get Down   92

17. Mind Power   103

18. Keeping It Movin'   108

19. The Hop   113

20. Push It Along   124

21. Scenario   134

22. Get A Hold   145

23. Steppin It Up   151

24. Enough!!   158

25. Rock Rock Y'all   167

26. Rumble in the Jungle   176

27. Money Maker   184

28. The Pressure   193

29. Crew   201

30. Keep it Rollin   209

31. Phony Rappers   220

32. God Lives Through   227

33. The Chase, Pt. II   234

34. Separate/ Together   246

35. Glamour and Glitz   252

36. Show Business   264

37. Award Tour   273

38. Hey   286

INSIDE LOOKING IN

FOREWORD

By

Arlen Dewaine Griffen aka "Griffy 2Trillion"

What's CRACKIN my name is Arlen Dewaine Griffin but since I was about 9 or so people just call me "GRIFF"!!! I'm a comedian, On-Air Personality, author, motivational speaker BLAH BLAH BLAH but this is not about me this is about one of my favorite people on the planet.

I could not be more honored to have been picked to piece together this foreword because everything has a beginning. I just happened to be at the beginning of this brother's career, and I saw it firsthand but the special thing between him and I is 'I CALLED IT!!' I KNEW what he was about to be and what he was working on becoming but I digress.

With more than 26 years in this entertainment business, I've seen a lot … but I just want to tell you two stories I saw so you can understand it in its actual perspective.

Story Number One:

Around the beginning of 2002 I hosted Beyonce's first Pay Per View which was a huge deal in Dearborn, Michigan that month because it was also the 100th Anniversary of FORD so in front of

100,000 people I watched from the side as Beyonce did her first show without Destiny's Child (who she closed out the show with) but this show was just about B!

When she was performing 'Crazy in Love' the plan was to have JAY-Z jump on stage and do his verse with her unbeknownst to the HUGE CROWD in Michigan. Well, Jigga wasn't on the premises yet and they were freaking out in my ear. (I'll explain why they were in my ear; mine AND Beyonce's because I can hear everything that she can hear) If you ever watch a news reporter or someone on tv doing their thing they have a wire hooked up to their ear that looks very much like a secret service walkie talkie but what it really is, is a direct line to the Producers booth; so they can tell you to 'skip that story' or 'stretch it out more.'

So, in my actual ear I can hear all these people panicking saying 'Jay's not gonna make it ... she's almost done with the song.' And then ... '4 Black SUV's are at the gate, let'em through, let'em through' ... 'He's not gonna make it in time' ... 'Tell her to go to the next song' ... 'wait the trucks are at the stage' and like a movie or video I've never seen before, Jay-Z gets out of the second truck by himself, walks right past me, grabs the mic from the lady who is also next to me and walks out in front of 100,000 screaming fans without missing a beat or running or walking fast at all just as casual like he was standing next to me back stage the whole time ... "Young Hov, y'all know when the flow is loco, young B and the R-O-C uh oh ..." The CROWD WENT BEYOND BANANAS ... fade to black.

<u>Story Number Two:</u>

In the early 2000's I was hosting this room at this spot-on Franklin Road, in Marietta Georgia called CAFÉ RED TRAIN (most people who remember it just call it 'The Train') it was owned by a Korean guy named Kevin who was one of the NON-ENGLISH SPEAKINGEST humans I'd ever met lol but he knew black people were coming to his spot and he was making money, so he was cool. On Wednesday's we called it the "GRIFFY2K COMEDY GONG SHOW" DJ Cowboy and I would host this thing to the tee … it was soooo hood, that it was amazing! Later DJ Silverknight would take over and then DJ T-WREX but in the beginning it was just me and Cowboy!

Wednesdays always went like this, I would come out and be funny get people ready, shout out all the birthdays …then we would bring on a comedian (mostly big names who were getting ready to come to Atlanta to perform THURS-SUN; I just told them to come pick up some bread at this REALLY HARD room on Franklin Road). After the comedian I would introduce my judges, it was always an athlete, and an entertainer and then the comedian …then we would start the show (note: Darius Rucker of Hootie and The Blowfish came to Café Red Train and BOMBED so not a fun room if you sucked) We made people pay to get on the list and then we would just run it … most people would get gonged …but sometimes there were gems on a Wednesday.

One particular Wednesday this young cat who really looked like he was 14 (and he only JUST now looks like he's 25 SMH) introduced himself, said he was from Virginia and CRUSHED the show (won the $100.00 for the night and I thought I would never see him again) but he came back every Wednesday and he won like ALL THE TIME, every Wednesday … after 2/3 Wednesdays of him getting this bread, I started making him freestyle … so I would literally say 'Talk about that ladies horrible wig, Kevin needing a better security and the dude that got gonged earlier' and he would never miss a beat and it was NEVER written … EVER!!!

So fast forward to everybody losing to MISTER every week. Kevin encourages me to have like a championship of this night so he can basically make more money … so we gave away $1000.00 to whoever could rock the mic the best! MISTER's parents fly in from V-A, they're the third most JESUSEY people I've ever met in my life, third behind Erica Campbell from the group Mary Mary and CeCe Winans. They come to this club that definitely aint the church, unless your church smells like weed, has prostitutes and dope boys playing pool, an easy THIRD of the people there had warrants but they had some dope chicken wings (I heard … never had'em, I've had 7/8 wings ever but back to the story)

MISTER asks me all TENDER 'can you keep the language down because of my parents?' and I tell him real slow so he can understand "HELL NAW! Your parents is at the Train … they gone be good!" In front of his parents and a historically thick night at the club MISTER won it all … but it wasn't him winning at the train it was him always pretending that he was on a stage somewhere around the world (that's how I warmed him up) he had IT and THAT is what Da BRAT saw when she was a judge one night at Café Red Train and the rest is HIS-STORY …

What an amazing MAN OF GOD and father MISTER is … I couldn't be more proud of the Homie!!! These memoirs will encourage you and test your faith but in the end it all comes down to who can rock the mic … and MISTER is an ATL LEGEND! (period)

"GRIFF"

Introduction

I never knew what it was like to really have a "day one," but I consider MR.… That guy. I met him at a club called Café Red Train in Marietta Georgia and he was the freestyle murderer. He slayed anybody that crossed his path. I wanted to be a part of making him a success, so I introduced myself…Not knowing that there was a full story of him meeting me before.

We started working together in the studio doing songs and eventually I asked him to come on the road with me to be my hype man on my tours. We have years of stories and memories on trying to make things happen with his career, starting labels, and helping other artist's that he had introduced me to.

Before MR. came into my life, I had shut the doors to letting anyone new in because my trust had been betrayed by so many others. But because I trusted MR. so much as we grew more fond of each other, I started to open myself up to the people that he had introduced me to. Because if he trusted them, I knew I could trust them. He knew me well and was clear on who I would not want around me. Most of those same people are still in my life today and have proven to be loyal and humble friends.

MR. has been down with me through thick and thin, from top to bottom and back to the top. His loyalty and drive to succeed remains unmatched by any artist or person I've ever worked with. I was very hard on MR. because I knew he had it in him. He has lived my life with me for years and has experienced some of the greatest moments you can imagine, from meeting top-notch stars to traveling to the most exotic places in different countries all over the globe.

We have definitely hit a few rough patches but by the grace of God we are still here together, surviving and mastering whatever craft we decide to involve ourselves in. He is the definition of a survivor and a dedicated warrior who is determined to be something great in this lifetime. And whatever his endeavors are, I will remain right by his side in whatever capacity I am needed. He believed in me when many others doubted. He rode it out with me no matter what. He a REAL ONE...MY DAY ONE. Ladies and gentlemen... Meet Mister Lavon Overstreet.

Shawntae "Da Brat" Harris

Prologue

My stomach is turning. There is no bathroom to run to, it's too late. I'm pacing back and forth, holding farts in, because God forbid, I ruin my underwear at a time like this. The hairs on my arm are at attention, with chill bumps all over. I'm handed a cordless microphone and my anxiety goes into overdrive. My eyes start to water. I can feel my heart racing. I feel a panic attack coming.

Now, I'm scared and not exactly sure that I'm doing a good job of hiding it. I'm feeling very alone. It's literally minutes before we hit that stage; the crowd is so loud that the screams and cheers give off the sound of a distant blend of "haahhhh". In the midst of all that, I pulled the cell phone out of my pocket and called my mother. She answered, thank God! I remember her asking me where I was. I had kept her informed everywhere I was going, each time I boarded a plane, so she was aware I was on the tour. I told her that at this present moment, I'm on the side of the stage, about to go on and…just came out with it, "Mom, I'm scared…can you please pray for me". Without a second to waste, my mom goes "Father, in the name of Jesus…". I pressed the phone into my ear and used the other hand that was holding the cordless, to plug my other ear. I tuned out everything that was going on around me, while my mother prayed for me on the phone. The way the prayer started, ended the same way, "…in Jesus name, Amen".

I thanked my mom and she encouraged me to do what I was born to do and that she loved me. We ended the call just in time to hear the host announce the next act. "Yall make some noise for…"!! Everything slows down and goes silent for me. I can feel my heart pounding and can hear myself breathing. I take a deep inhale, as I make my way up the steps. This is it.

Start It Up

Growing up, the people we heard on the radio, were gods in a sense. Meaning, never, at any point in our lives, would we have anything to do with these artists personally. We wouldn't see them in our day to day. They're not coming over for cookouts and we're not really bumping into them at the local grocery store. It's like music artists were not of this world. That's how much we were detached from them. The only time we would have any chance of experiencing them, was thru hearing them on the radio or paying for the experience by seeing them in concert, which for most people, was a once in a lifetime type of activity.

Anybody that I had heard on the radio, or saw on television, was not of this world. They were part of a dream world, a fantasy world. I always wondered…how did they get inside the radio? Or, how did they get inside the TV? These types of people were different and very special, aliens maybe. I remember thinking to myself, "I wanna be in the radio, I wanna to be on TV." Just how do I do that? Is it even possible for a regular person like me? So, let's *Start It Up*, where do I begin?

Let me see…The Year was 1994. The place, the Hampton Coliseum in Hampton, VA. Legendary Hip Hop group, A Tribe Called Quest is headlining. The energy in the city is crazy! The line is wrapped around the building but wait! Before I get into that, let's rewind just a bit to where this journey all began. A journey, where the aim is to make the transition from

MISTER

viewing the music industry from the outside, to actually a front row seat
Inside, Looking In.

8 Million Stories

For most of my life, I was raised as a military brat, constantly moving from one place to another, city to city, state to state, even out of the country. Basically, these travels would have our family living on the East Coast, West Coast, to down South, and overseas. It's because of this upbringing, that I'm able to adapt pretty quickly to change and adjust to any environment I'm placed in. It seemed like every other year, it was pick up and go, during my childhood and I sponged off of the culture in every place that we moved to.

Most people, I would learn, have an attachment to where they're "from" and usually embody that culture in the form of a certain attitude, slang, fashion, and taste. In my case, not so much. Though I was born in the rural area of Polk County, Florida, and lived there until I was six years old, I didn't retain much of the culture, as opposed to the rest of my family who were raised there all of their lives.

I would get teased when we would go back to visit, about how "proper" I talked, as opposed to having this deep southern drawl. Trust me, there is a huge difference, while in conversation, to pronounce words to sound like "street", instead of "skreet" or "put that back" instead of "put that bike". You'll stand out pretty quick off of dialogue alone. This doesn't help in trying to fit in, at all.

I say all of this to say, that I don't consider myself ever having a dedicated look, slang, or taste that's tied to one particular region. My personality is shaped from all of the places I've ever lived. With me, ain't no telling what you'd get. You're liable to hear some Down South slang, with a mixture of an Up North accent, while rocking a tilted ball cap, reciting an Ice Cube verse word for word.

On any given day, you would think I'm from just about anywhere. There's a blended assortment of behavior and style that you would notice I have, but none of them stand out more than the influence I got from Virginia.

By the time I got to Virginia, I was a pre-teen and spent my entire adolescent years to young adulthood there, which is how I retained most of that culture from the region we termed the Middle East. My dad ended up stationed at Fort Lee, Virginia, which was in the small town of Petersburg.

This city was about twenty minutes away from its "big brother" city of Richmond. It is the home of NBA great, Moses Malone, Hollywood actors, Blair Underwood and Tim Reid. It also the hometown of R&B singer, Trey Songz. Not far from there, was also where R&B/Pop sensation, Chris Brown, grew up.

Great people, good weather, and fun can be found year-round in this small town that also housed the HBCU, Virginia State University. However, Crime was at an all-time high in Richmond during these years and the street constituents of Petersburg were fighting just as hard to not be overshadowed. Murder, robbery, and drug sales was the climate, with very little else to do or room to avoid action, in a small town. You didn't have to look for trouble at all...it was right there at SouthPark mall, school, church, the skating rink, the local parks, even Wal-Mart.

So, the career path outside that of crime, was similar to most; play sports, graduate and go to college, graduate and work at one of the many warehouses or tobacco plants that were everywhere in the area, or join the military. Being a Rapper, or having a career in the music industry was just something that wasn't discussed as an option. That would definitely fall under the topic of being a dream for most, similar to hitting the lottery. This is mainly because we hardly knew of anyone, personally, that was even good enough to do it. Back then, everyone wasn't able to actually rap or perceived talented on the scale of what we were hearing on the radio or seen on TV. If you knew how to rhyme, it was a huge deal, and you could count on one hand, the amount of people you actually knew that can rhyme. If you did, you were definitely an exceptional person walking around and people would ask you to do it often. Very different era.

I tell you man, growing up in Virginia, or "VA", what we called it, is an entire book within itself. I grew into a man there and would experience everything from police brutality, going to jail, witnessing murders, shootouts, getting into huge brawls in and outside of school, both drug using and selling, you name it.

This type of life is much the norm for most black people, growing up in America. The odd part, is that, you just wouldn't expect such an upbringing for someone with both parents in the household, raised in the church, and living as a military brat. Being raised in VA was quite an adventure, like for real. With that said, I'll reserve much of the details for that book at another time, a bestseller for sure.

MISTER

Well, with so much drama going on in Virginia, I never paid much attention to rapping. That was until, my friend Larry asked me to rap with him at church. We both attended Mt. Olivet Baptist Church off of Halifax and Market streets in downtown Petersburg, where both of our dads were ministers. Yep, we were what you called "PK, preacher kids". Most people know the reputation of preacher kids being of the worst kind. It's something about being raised with a foundation of 'knowing better', being taught the 'going to Hell' consequences of such actions, yet intentionally going out and doing the exact opposite of abiding by the Christian lifestyle.

Larry, better known as Lil Larry, is, by far, one of my closest partners in crime. Though we went to the same church, he lived in another neighborhood opposite of mine. Our sides didn't really click with each other, so we initially just knew of each other, but not really associate like that. We ended up getting cool, because I had started dating his sister. I really think his plan was to befriend me, just to keep me away from her.

In a way, it kind of worked, cuz we were pretty much inseparable, growing up. We were both similar in height, shared a lot of the same interests, and could relate to each other, far as what we had to go thru growing up in a Christian household. We both, also, were highly attracted to the street life and just wanting to break the chains of being sheltered at home. This dude also had game like no other and could talk his way in and out of any situation, especially when it came to girls.

There has to be about *8 Million Stories* I can tell about everything me and Larry have gotten into. Most of the dirt I've ever been involved in, has been alongside my guy and it's safe to say that we committed a great deal of these sins right there inside the house of God. Our church was like one of those mega churches, that easily housed hundreds, maybe even over a thousand people in it, which made it the biggest church in Petersburg.

We even had the camera services, where the church service would be filmed and tapes would be sold. Me and Larry even worked the cameras sometimes on Sundays. It was fun, because we would zoom in on people digging up their noses, and from the balcony, we could zoom in on the top of some of the ladies, looking at their cleavage. That would be until the camera director would call us out and let us know that we're "hot", meaning our camera was live at the moment. Why they gave us cameras to operate, was beyond me. They knew our reputation for cutting up in the church.

Another one of our favorite things to do, was to sit visibly in the church pews, up in the balcony area, so that our parents could see us get seated, and once church started, we were ducking out of there and hanging out on the block. Sometimes, we would go up in other churches, that were in the area, to find girls. We'd wait until they ask for all visitors to "please stand". We'd stand up, just to be seen and scope out the area, but as soon as that sermon was about to start, we was out!

Most likely, we'd head to the corner store to kick it with Papoose, who was an infamous figure in da Burg. He was a midget that hung out in the streets, that everybody knew and knew about all of the drama that was happening in the streets. We would kick it with him for a minute, cracking jokes and picking fights with the homeless dudes, then hit up Hardee's Chicken. Before our church service was over, we would be back in time for the Benediction. Those were crazy times man! But, hey, enough of incriminating myself with the Lord right now. Besides, it's not like he doesn't know anyway, but He knows my heart.

Anyhow, there was some kind of event being held at the church and they asked Larry to rap. Larry was in a rap group called Swat Team with two other guys from around the way that we were cool with named Mike and Pooh. They were one of the few guys that were known to rap around the neighborhood and even made it to Richmond to record a couple of tracks at the studio, which was a big deal back then.

In addition to rapping, Mike and Pooh, both were heavily involved in the streets, so a great deal of the crime and street drama came along with them. Pooh and I lived in the same neighborhood, while Mike and Larry lived on the other side, just off of the base in a notorious area called Jackson Circle. Like I said earlier, we all didn't get along at first, and would have a few clashes at the basketball courts, parks, and the Y. Going to the same church, brought me and Larry together as friends first. Having aligned enemies in the street, along with being one of the few that can rap, would lead Mike and Pooh to getting cool. All of this led to the rap group being formed by these guys.

A few years prior, back when I lived in Texas, I had learned to write rhymes and performed them with a group of friends at recess, but it was more of an experimental thing that I definitely didn't consider taking serious at the moment. After I moved and relocated to Virginia, I hadn't given writing any rhymes a second thought. So, at this particular time, I wasn't rapping at all and not even closely considered to being a part of the group, so I admired them from the outside like everyone else.

With that said, it was Larry who had come up with this whole church rap for us to perform and he wanted me to do the second verse. I thought it would be fun to rap again, so I agreed to do it. I remember practicing for it a lot and when the time came to put it down on that Friday evening at the church, we KILLED it!! The congregation was up on their feet, clapping, and all into it. We did a rendition of EPMD's song that was on the airwaves then, called "Crossover".

"Whatever you want, uh huh…whatever you need, hey hey
My Jesus can do…lift Christ up"

Man, you couldn't tell us nothing!! We flipped the radio joint and turned it into a church song with ease and had the entire congregation going crazy. The way we took a secular song and conformed it to a Christian jingle, was something that was never heard of before, or at least we hadn't seen it done that way. This was way before a guy named Kirk Franklin called himself doing it. They liked it so much that the pastor of the church, Rev. McLaughlin, asked us to perform it again at the main service on Sunday. Asking us to perform at the main service, was like moving from performing at a kid's talent show to Showtime at the Apollo!

Back to the show, my nerves were so bad to get in front of all these people and rhyme. Though we had just did it on that Friday before, it was different because it was less people in the congregation. Needless to say, we pulled off the encore in even better fashion. I remember it well...we both rocked black jeans, black T's that read REAL MEN DON'T FAINT, fitted starter caps, and sneakers. I had on a pair of the Nike Fab Five Huarache's and Larry had on the Tim Hardaway Air Raids. We had the youth choir backing us up and everything! Yo, it was crazy and one hell of a rush!

Man, the feeling of holding that microphone, hearing my voice amplified thru the speakers, watching everyone's faces in amazement, singing along to the catchy hook we made, and just having a great time, is almost indescribable. It's something about having a crowd of people doing what you tell them to do, waving their hands from side to side, I mean, it was like we were on our own pulpit at the moment, delivering our own Word, and the spirit was moving! It was such an exhilarating experience that I'll never forget.

We received a standing ovation and after the service, everybody was coming up to us and praising our performance. Everyone was so proud of us, including our parents, which was a big deal, because my parents certainly hated that 'rap mess'. This showed them that it wasn't all that bad. There was plenty of excitement around our performance, but the one thing that people kept asking was 'who wrote the song?' Larry would say, "I wrote it". That would lead to everyone asking how he was able to do such a thing, like putting the rhymes together like that.

Like I said, having the talent to rap, was a very rare thing. The fact that Larry had just written an entire song, both his verse and mine, was a great feat. Not only can he write something for himself, but it was phenomenal enough to where he was even able to write a verse for me and turn me into a rapping talent. If you never asked, you would think that I wrote the verse myself. It wasn't enough for me to get praises for the rap performance alone, I wanted to be able to show that I'm talented enough to write my own rhymes too. It was at that moment, I decided to write again!

Da Crib…207 Yorktown Drive, Ft. Lee, VA

MISTER

Can I Kick It

No one had known me to rap in VA, because I had put it all down after I left Texas. I decided to go home and write a rap verse. I remember vividly sitting at home, using my mom's word processer to type the lyrics out. It was the same word processer that I used to type out lyrics to rap songs that I heard on the radio, just so I could learn them and recite them like the rest of my peers.

Again, the big deal, with that, was the fact that I grew up in a strict Christian household. Rap music was not allowed in my home. So, all the rap music that I've mentioned I was a fan of, was heard on the radio or on dubbed cassettes that I listened to when my parents weren't home. Or I would listen to these songs when at my friend's homes that were allowed to listen to it all day. With that, I wouldn't know all the songs that everybody else knew, so I would have to listen to them when I could and write or type the lyrics down, so I could memorize them in order to fit in when my peers would recite them at school, outside, or on the bus. Funny right? I know.

What I didn't realize, was that I was building a skill set of learning to memorize rhymes, practice rhyme patterns, and learning what the public wants to hear. So, on this same word processer, I decided to type out my first rhyme after about a three-year layoff.

Here I am, hiding out in the hallway closet of the house, amongst stacks of copy paper, books, blankets, and other stored household items, on this word processer. I'm concentrating and giving my all to come up with the best verse ever. There's a lot of coming up with something and hitting the backspace over and over, being satisfied and dissatisfied with what I was coming up with. It took me hours to come up with what was about eight bars of lyrics. After going over it multiple times, I had settled on what I was sure to be the hottest verse around. I was so excited about it, that I printed it, ripped it out, folded it in my pocket, walked around the neighborhood, and recited it for days.

I remember running into Pooh out in the streets and telling him that I wanted to be down with Swat Team. I, basically, told him that I just wrote this verse that I thought was pretty dope and asked, "*Can I Kick It*" for him? He was like, "Let me hear it." See, getting Pooh to cosign my rap is huge, because he was one of the best rhymers around. His approach was aggressive and had that type of big boy rap that matched his physique.

Pooh was one of the first guys that I met when I moved to VA and he played a great part in keeping me away from a lot of the street stuff that was happening. Pooh was very live and ran with a crew of dudes in our neighborhood that was constantly in the mix. He had a reputation for being about that action, as well as the rest of the guys in our area. We would say he resembled the rapper, Grand Puba of Brand Nubians, because from the haircut and style of dress, they were damn near twins. Pooh was one of the first to have a car, as well as one of the first to carry a gun.

See, the thing to do then, was hanging. Hanging consisted of being out late, riding out with the rest of the gang, going to different hoods, getting high, basically, just slanging and banging. In the early days of me being in

VA, I was never allowed to hang out with these types of guys and definitely not get into the types of activities they were involved in. For one, it was very difficult to hang with a curfew of 815pm and second, my parents would kill me. A lot of times, I had to get creative and say that I was going to the movies, with some friends, in order to stay out past curfew. My parents found out, quickly, the difference between my 'good' friends and my 'thug' friends.

Since Larry went to church with us, he was definitely considered one of the good guys that I could say I was going to hang with. Pooh, on the other hand, not so much. That was ruined when he came to pick me up from the house once, and my parents swore they saw him trying to hide a brown paper bag, behind the seat.

Regardless, me and Pooh became friends, so being close to the drama was inevitable. Whenever there were some real things about to pop off, he would be one of the main people to tell me to take it to the house and to not get involved, or just not let me get in the ride to go anywhere with them. Pooh knew my parents and even more, knew me. I was a smart, cool guy and it wouldn't make sense to be out screwing my life up, by doing "dumb shit." In hindsight, it was much appreciated, although it didn't pan out too well for me in that area anyway. It's good to know, that contrary to what my parents thought, those "thugs" I was out hanging with, actually cared and tried to tell me better.

I had other motives as a teen. Those motives had an end game of being part of the gang. For me, it was a very challenging period in my life. I was very immature, peer pressure was thick, and I was the new kid on the block, yet again. Being neutral and minding your own business is cool, but it was also mad boring. I had a need to Belong, to get in the mix, to be the topic of street gossip and school conversations.

It wasn't enough that I was already a popular kid, my name alone, is responsible for that. Having a name like 'Mister', spread like fire, with everyone wanting to know who I was. I quickly became one of the 'cool kids' and got along with everybody, no matter what side you lived on. I did nerd things, like being a member of the chess club and was also in band. Even still, I got a lot of attention from the girls as being "so cute", which was cool, but "cute" will only get you to first base most of the time. The phrase 'nice guys finish last' was a real one and let's just say these bad guys were hitting home runs out the park.

My immature way of thinking would prevail, and it wasn't long before I had quit both the band and the chess club, and migrated to being one of the bad boys. One of the ways I saw myself getting integrated into that crowd was by getting down with Pooh and this rap crew. This would be an In. It can be argued that the streets was the first 'Inside' that I was actually looking to get in prior to the music game. In my mind, back then, if I wasn't going to rap, I just wanted to be a gangster.

Looking back, it all makes sense and has similar gratification, with the common denominators being that of popularity, more money, different level of social circles, and what else, more girls! At the time, movies like "Colors", "Menace II Society, "Boyz N The Hood", "King of New York", and "Juice" were very magnetizing. I mean, I would literally ride around and play nothing but NWA, Cube, Onyx, Kool G Rap, and Scarface as background music to set the mood each day. Hip Hop culture and the media definitely influences the behavior for a lot of kids, no matter how much you try to instill them with anything different. "So, pass the 40 and put on that Wutang...Bring Da Muthafukin Rukus."

Kicking this rhyme for Pooh would be my first audition to find my way into this rap crew and an In to hanging more, getting into the mix. I kicked the verse for him like I was rapping for an executive at Def Jam records. He listened, grinning the whole time, as if he knew my hidden agenda, then said it was good. I think I shocked him that I was actually decent. He said he would get with Mike and Larry to see what's up with me getting down. I knew I had Larry in my corner, but Mike was another story.

If there was ever anybody that I knew of, since a kid, that exemplified the characteristics of being Gangster, it was Michael Lundy. The irony was that this guy had to be about 140lbs soaking wet and loved the action. Any talk around the town of a fight, shootout, or just any crazy story in general, most likely had the name Michael Lundy attached to it. Guys from my neighborhood, like Pooh, and a host of others would have run-ins with Mike and his crew often. The clashes were monumental, and the stories are nothing short of entertainment at its best.

I personally ended up on the bad end of an altercation that he and I had, after running into him and a couple of his homies one night. Our issue stemmed from my girlfriend, which again, was Larry's sister. Before she and

MISTER

I hooked up, I remember her for talking to him awhile back. Mike felt that I took her from him and let's just say that he didn't take it too well.

After a while of going back and forth between his side and mine, it would be Larry to eventually make the peace between us. At the end of the day, we all had similar enemies to which it made more sense for us to be on the same team, as opposed to trying to hurt each other. Cooler heads would prevail and had us all being the best of friends eventually, even to this day.

In addition to playing basketball, slanging, and banging, Mike, just like Pooh, could rap! He was very good at it, so good, that everyone was certain that if anybody could get a record deal, it would be him. Mike and Pooh were the first to team up and start rapping around the city together. With Larry being Mike's close friend, he brought him into the fold, so to me, it only made sense that I get down too! So, as it was, after kicking my verse for Pooh, the rest of the group would call me, three way, and I would kick the rhyme again over the phone. Mike and Larry gave their blessings, and I was officially part of Swat Team.

It's on and popping now! I'm getting calls from Mike, the self-appointed leader of the crew, telling me to write verses for different titles he came up with. We would later change the group name to Black Masked Assassins! Black Masked Assassins were Cock D (Mike), Dynamite (Pooh), Quizik (Larry), and me, Sydekick aka Tech9. We had songs called, "Tales From the Ghetto", "Back to the Lab", "Return of The Roughneck", and of course, "Black Masked Assassins".

These songs were all written, but not recorded. We didn't have the resources of a recording studio, so all of the songs were just written and performed everywhere for friends at the basketball courts, on the street corner, rundown apartment buildings, and projects in the middle of drug sells and gun play.

Running around with the Swat Team, had me officially 'hanging' now, doing things my parents would have a heart attack for, if they knew. I mean, seriously, I don't even know how I made it home alive a lot of times and can't recall too many times coming home sober. These were wild times man.

In the midst of the wild, criminal, and teenage activity, the focus was still on trying to make some noise with this rap thing. I remember we rehearsed for what seemed like weeks for this big talent show that was going down at Petersburg High School. We were performing Black Masked Assassins over the "Scenario Remix" beat by my favorite group at the time, A Tribe Called Quest featuring Leaders of the New School and Kid Hood.

We were ready to kill it and I was ready to show my fellow crewmembers that I was more than ready. We all rocked hoodies with skullcaps on. I had the purple hoodie, with the purple Naughty by Nature skully on. You know, the skullcap with the string that tied around the top. Yeahhh, that joint! I have to admit, after walking in that high school's auditorium and seeing people from all over the city, even from Richmond down there, I was nervous as hell. I kept practicing and practicing the verses over and over in my head, trying to block the crowd noise out, but on the inside, bubble guts. We literally had just walked in the auditorium and stage fright was in overdrive. I did my best to stay to myself and not show it.

MISTER

Mike had a cousin named Diante who was in a group that was doing their thing in the hood. They had a white boy DJ named Casper who was ill. I remember at the show they came out on stage with the Jason masks on…ohhhh, that shit was ill! As luck would have it, at least for my sake, the inevitable happened. Some ruckus popped off and we weren't able to get on stage and rock that night. Don't ask me why, but I was relieved! I wasn't really 100% confident that I wouldn't forget my verse, which was the FIRST verse at that. I was experiencing crazy butterflies and some serious bouts of anxiety due to the stage fright. This, I would find out later, is something that I would never get rid of. We never made it to a public platform like that again to do our thing as a group.

We continued rhyming amongst our peoples and out in the projects for thrills. We even had the younger homies doing their thing. Pooh had a little brother named Dre, who hung with a bunch of other wild kids, that hung and played basketball. With all of the hysteria surrounding us doing our rap thing, they decided to jump in as well. This ended up with me and Pooh writing rhymes for Dre and his crew to show out and perform for their friends at local parties. That provided me with my first experience writing for someone else and it felt good to see the results. Especially hearing all of the chatter about how dope Dre and his crew was on the rhyme tip.

Given all of the obstacles we had, it still seemed like we had a little bit of momentum, by the buzz we were getting. Having a buzz was cool and all, but the distractions were still prevalent. As much as we were all into different types of mischief, Mike and Pooh were heavily active in the streets, so keeping them focused on music wasn't so easy. With them, it was basically 'bullets over bars.' Things were getting very real and I kept a level head in doing my best to stay out of the way of the next murder or drug raid.

The atmosphere at home was getting worse due to the amount of trouble I was starting to get in. I started to get disrespectful with my behavior at home, talking back, skipping school, ditching church, to kick it on the block, in church clothes, sneaking in and out of the house thru my bedroom window. It was a very rebellious time for me.

Even though I was making a lot of dumb decisions, I wasn't dumb by far. With all of the craziness going on, at this point, I pretty much knew that I wasn't trying to be a gangster for the rest of my life. Hell, I was witnessing close hand how that lifestyle is not for me. Sure, a lot of it is a rush, with some great perks, but it's just flat out dangerous. I keep this up, I'll be dead or in jail, for sure.

That's not me and it's not what my parents raised me to be. It's time I smarten up. We out here running into obstacle after obstacle with this rap thing and the outcome is not looking promising. Overall, I need to make wiser choices, as it relates to my future.

MISTER

Larry

Mike Lundy (with Ronski)

Pooh

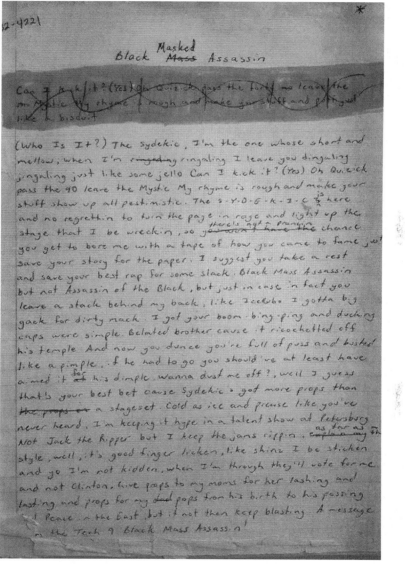

Verse from "Black Masked Assassin" for the Peterburg HS talent show

MISTER

Motivators

The summer before my Senior year in High School, I found myself in El Paso, Texas, as part of boot camp for the military. Larry's dad was a recruiter for the National Guard and would post up at the school, handing out cool pencils and notepads during lunch, trying to talk us into joining.

Being that he was my girlfriend's dad, I felt that he would particularly lean on me extra hard to make something of my life. He promised that I would get thousands of dollars just for joining and it would only be on a part time basis. I used to entertain him on the regular, mainly because I just wanted to be in his good graces. After all, I was dating his daughter, it was the least I could do. I also thought it would be a way to score points with my own parents by showing them that I do have a plan for my future, despite the trouble I was getting into.

My parents weren't really with it at all, but after a few more instances of me getting in trouble at school and out in the streets, they eventually signed the paperwork to have me shipped off to boot camp.

I arrived at boot camp, as this 17-year-old knucklehead, thinking I could get by with how I was acting on the streets. By the time I stepped off that bus and had a duffle bag thrown at me, I knew it was real. I spent the first couple of weeks being disruptive as hell, getting into fights, and talking back to the drill sergeants, until finally these grown men had enough and let's just say I was put in my place.

These *Motivators* somehow had a unique way of transforming hard heads to humble creatures, to which I had a head of cement, that quickly was turned to humble pie. Feeling defeated and broken, I would end up crying in my pillow at my bunk, wishing I could go home. It wasn't long before it dawned on me to just get with the program and buy into what they were selling, which I did.

I made a complete turnaround and it led to me being the platoon guide, and the youngest, loudest, soldier in the bunch. My nickname was "Mouthpiece", while most called me by my last name, "Street". Of course, I was all the way out at boot camp, kicking rhymes for everybody and showing off my skills. It was one of the places where I could really practice more on my writing too.

It wasn't long before I found a way to sneak off base and into the city, just to make it back with some contraband, which was a handheld cassette player. I would stash it in my cargo pockets for when I had guard duty in the middle of the night. Me and another soldier would just sit with our M16s, watching the stars, while listening to the cassette I had bought of Pete Rock and CL Smooth, called "Mecca and the Soul Brother". They had this record called "When They Reminisce Over You", which is one of my all-time favorites. It's the only cassette I had bought, so I would listen to it on repeat during my entire time at boot camp.

That tape player, the phone calls, and letters got me thru that summer and it wasn't long before I was back home, showing off with how many push-ups I could do in two minutes. The things that I went thru in boot camp, only made my overall bravado worse, so I came back mentally and physically stronger, but would still succumb to the pressures of the chaos that awaited me back in VA.

No one cared that I went off and tried to make something of myself by joining the National Guard, it was business as usual. The heat was still on out in the streets and I found myself deep in the middle of it. A lot of the drama just came my way, because of the history that I had already created and the friends that I chose to run with. The seeds were planted, and the beef doesn't go anywhere.

Pvt. Mister Overstreet aka "Street" aka "Mouthpiece"

Fort Bliss, Texas...located in El Paso

Pad & Pen

The summer was officially over and school is back in session at Prince George High School. For most of my friends, we were all seniors and excited about this being our last year at school. There's nothing like the first day of school, or the first week for that matter. I remember they had all of the seniors take a class photo in the front of the school during that first week. It's crazy that the crew in the corner of the photo would all end up not graduating. That crew being me and my friends.

I mean, it's almost as if, school was just the meeting grounds for our very own OK Corral! It didn't take long for the drama to pop off. It literally took days! Long story short, Mike ended up getting kicked out of school for fighting, caught numerous cases, and landed in jail. Pooh ended up getting kicked out of school for getting caught with a gun in the school, was charged, and eventually landed in jail. Larry ended up getting kicked out of school for selling drugs, turned to hustling, and just quit rapping altogether.

Me, on the other hand, was still hanging on by a thread and had settled to entertaining friends like my homie, Al, at the lunch table with every new rhyme I would come up with. Al lived in my neighborhood as well, but with all of the nerd components and smarts that I had, Al was actually the wise friend, with the most sense. He literally had his career mapped out in high school on what he wanted to do and how he was going to do it. His focus was admirable. This lover of the rap group, Public Enemy, and The Geto Boys, was the guy who would keep me levelheaded and make me feel like a complete dummy with the choices I was making out in the streets, with wanting to get Active and hang.

Al is the type of person who I did most of my fun mischief with, which mostly consisted of girl chasing and just kicking it. He was completely not sold on me being the thug I had become and definitely not sold on me being a rapper. To him, I'm just the same little kid, who had just quit the band, member of the chess club, that loved strawberry shortcake ice cream that came on a stick. Rapper? Get out of here! Hands down, Al is my biggest rap critic!

The lunch table at school was where most of my bars were heard for the first time with Al and our lunch crew. I struck out more than I impressed these guys and it would motivate me to consistently try and come up with something they would approve of. As I mentioned, most of my crew had been kicked out of school already, so I was the lone ranger remaining and for the most part, I was just trying to stay out of the way.

I mentioned that I was hanging on by a thread, because I had gotten into a little bit, well a lot, of trouble shortly after my crew was kicked out. Some things that happened out in the streets, spilled over into me being the subject of payback at the school later. This led to the school placing me on a disciplinary contract after my participation in a brawl, where I smashed a chair over someone's head. I had been charged, went to jail, and was expelled.

After my parents pleading with the superintendent and having a prior clean record, I was reinstated to finish school. It also helped that academically, I was a straight A student, go figure. So now I'm back at school, but I'm on a contract where I can receive zero infractions. This was especially hard, because the guys that I was beefing with were still in the school and would antagonize me every day. My Christian ways of 'turning the other cheek' came into play quite often. Any fighting, or even a disruptive argument with any student, would be means for permanent expulsion. The best thing I could do was to mind my own business, which I desperately tried to do.

I would do nothing but sit in class and write rhymes all day! All I had was my *Pad & Pen*. Day in and day out, at school, I was jotting down lyrics in my notebooks. Being that I was a gifted student, academically, I didn't pay too much attention to what was going on in the classroom, as I was too busy formulating verses that I was anxious to kick for anyone who would listen.

One day I was caught writing lyrics, by a teacher in class, who sent me to detention in the principal's office. That led to them asking me to channel my writing talents by writing a song advertising the year's school Prom. I was shocked that they asked me to do it, but nevertheless, I knocked it out with ease. I wrote the verse, memorized it and to calm my nerves, smoked a blunt before school. I literally came in wreaking with the smell. Al called me out on it and ended up using some roll-on deodorant on my clothes to help with the odor. I know, I know…leave me alone about it.

The administrative staff didn't seem to notice and allowed me to go ahead and do my thing, in which I showed out! You know, giving shout outs to the whole crew and favorite teachers in the verses. They had me perform on the PA system before the start of 1st period, which was major. I got nothing but praise, which we called "props" back then, all day and all year after that. Outside of me actually being high, this experience had me on a different high. I was sure that I was heading down the right path with this thing. All I needed was more opportunities like I just had to get me noticed even more. I can do this!

Things were actually on the up and up, and appear to be changing for the better. The majority of my crew and most of the rivals was kicked out of school, so I wasn't distracted by the negative drama that came with that. Being on the contract at school, was kind of helping, in that it kept me focused on staying on the straight and narrow. I even had close friends of mine, like Al, and a crew of girlfriends that would look out for me, escort me to class, making sure I would stay out of trouble.

At home, I was more respectful and really working to impress my parents. Remember, I had just come back from boot camp, so I'm in the National Guard, got myself a couple thousand dollars. I grabbed a job at McDonald's as well, so I have some legal money in my pocket. Grades are good at school and I'm applying for colleges. I'm in a great relationship with my girlfriend. Outside of the little beefs I have at the school, I'm really cool with just about everyone still. I wasn't really getting tried by anyone like that. The notoriety is there for getting down, so there's a different level of respect by the real guys around.

To add the cherry on top, I'm now known as one of the few people that can actually rap and the only person to ever perform over the school PA system. I'm on my way man!

MISTER

It seems like when you're winning, the Devil gets extremely jealous and starts to work overtime. With all of the emotional highs that I was having, little did I know, my life was about to take a turn for the worse.

Senior class picture…that's me, Mike, and Larry on the left side in the front.

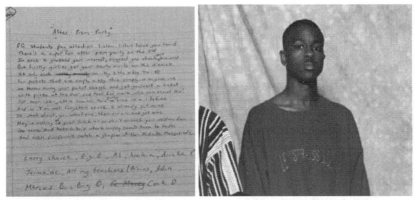

Verse for the Prom on PA System.   My best friend, Al

Stressed Out

Between the influence I was getting from my parents at home, then from Al, I was really getting focused. I'm pursuing my dream of making it as a rapper, while at the same time, making smart decisions for my future, by enrolling in the National Guard and applying for colleges. I feel that I'm doing everything right. Yet, it seems, the biggest motivating factor, responsible for my focus, was the first thing that was attacked.

I thought the school was on my side and supported my talent for rapping. I was wrong. Even with the remarkable job I did with writing the song for the school, I still would get in trouble for writing rhymes in class. I can't believe it! The very thing I was applauded for, I was being chastised for at the same time.

I can't make this up, literally for writing rhymes, it would land me in In-School Suspension, and even Out-of-School Suspension. I guess it doesn't matter that I'm on top of my studies, completing my work, passing my classes, scoring big on my tests, and not disturbing others at all. I admit, yes, harping on me about writing a rhyme, quietly, at my desk, would get me to snap. This is mainly, because I felt that they were picking on me and trying to make an example out of me for no reason.

It goes without saying too much, that the school I attended was also very racist. We had only one black administrator, who actually played for the other team. Mostly all of my teachers were white and personally, had it out for me. Especially once I was able to be reinstated for school. It was almost as if, they were disappointed that I was still in school after everything that had transpired with that brawl.

Don't get me wrong, I did have a few teachers, like my English teacher, Mr. Astin, who were an exception. He would ask me to talk with him after class and would tell me that he's not fooled by my class antics, knew I had more potential than I was letting on. Mr. Astin would send me home with the Finance section of the paper and teach me about stocks. I looked into it and was interested, but as soon as the other students caught wind that I was doing it, I immediately digressed, as being young and dumb made me believe that studying stocks was too nerdy and uncool. Man, how I wish I could turn back the hands of time now. Mr. Astin was literally showing me a way out.

It was teachers like him that really tried to look out for me, but the majority didn't. I really thought it was just petty to constantly come down on me for just writing. The older and more mature me, would recognize that it's all a mind game and to adapt. Hell, I had just learned those principles that summer while at boot camp. However, the younger and rebellious me, the passionate about Rap, me, the dislike for authority me, just wasn't having it. So, for every action, there's a reaction.

Remember, I'm on a contract, but the infractions did not involve any violence against other students or disruptions for that matter, so though I was getting written up for writing raps, it wasn't means to violate me altogether. It wasn't until I had an altercation with a guy that was stalking me the entire year, knowing that I was on a contract, provoking me at no end, that I was eventually kicked out of school myself.

Me and this guy had an ongoing beef, both inside and outside of the school. I ran into him outside of school one day when I was with Al. Not knowing his intentions, at the time, I pulled out my knife in an attempt to try and stab the guy. He made it to his car and got away before I could successfully do so. This dude then gets to the school and informs the administrator of the incident that happened outside of the school.

As chance would have it, I caught him in the hallway just after the bell rang for class and tried to fight him. I couldn't even get my bookbag off fast enough, before an administrator caught me in the act. "Hey, break it up…Mister Overstreet, that's it!" Just like that, it was over.

I was so angry and hurt, because I had made it almost an entire school year, under the worse conditions, dodging altercations, making good grades, accomplishing so much. It was to the point where I had already ordered a cap and gown, with graduation invites. Did they really have to kick me out? I mean, the situation that started this, didn't even happen on school grounds!

Ultimately, it was the one black administrator that actually expelled me. I begged him not to do it, but he didn't budge. I was so mad that I cursed him out and bolted out of the school building, walking up the street to head home, crying the whole way. To put it into perspective, graduation was in June, I was kicked out in May. At that moment, I had academic admissions for Hampton University, Syracuse University, and University of Miami. They all went out of the window with my expulsion.

Graduation went down on June 18th and I attended, as to appear that I wasn't bothered by the notion of not graduating. I went to see all of my friends walk across the stage, mainly my best friend Al. He actually did the right thing and refrained from the bs to make it out. I remember his dad, Mr. Wells, shaking my hand, with a smile on his face, saying, "yeah, you f*cked up". I see where Al gets his cynicism from and I got the message loud and clear. Inside I was crushed. They still had my name on the program of graduating seniors, but skipped over it on the program.

My parents were able to get me in good graces with the school and they allowed me to test out, so I was able to at least receive my high school diploma. To add more insult to injury, it was an Advanced Honors diploma, imagine that.

I just couldn't graduate and it honestly, hurt. I still sent out graduation invites to my family down in Florida. I figured it was still something that would make my grandparents and other family proud. I had disappointed my family on so many levels, making it not much to sing praises about, but at least getting the diploma was a slight accomplishment, given all that I did to try and ruin it.

Picture Day at Prince George High School, 12th Grade

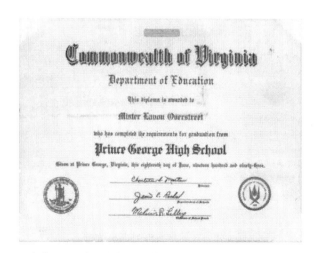

Advanced Diploma from Prince George HS

Lost Somebody

June 19th, the day after the high school graduation, was a great day! It's summertime in VA, which was always a blast. The weather is nice, sun is out, and I'm up getting ready to hit these streets and see what they talking about for the day.

While I'm in my room, getting dressed, my mother calls me into her room. I've already gone thru enough drama and was really *Stressed Out*. I'm thinking, "what did I do now", but she had a somber look on her face. She was seated next to the phone in her bedroom and asked me to sit down. The words from her mouth hit me like a sledgehammer. My daddy Kenny, my childhood hero and biological father, had just been killed in a car accident. I was completely stunned and numb at the same time. I cried, but not hysterically, just quietly while seated on my mother's bed.

I remember telling her that I just needed to take a walk. I walked outside on what was the most beautiful day out. As I'm walking thru the neighborhood, to the store, by the parks, it was like a whole world of fun was happening around me. An entire world of people who didn't have a clue as to what I was dealing with.

I was completely zoned out. Nothing mattered, not a girlfriend, not a diploma, church, hanging with the crew, Nothing, especially not Rap. I went from feelings of anger, regret, hurt, and sadness over and over. There's this song by an artist by the name of MC Brains, who had been discovered by Michael Bivins of New Edition/BBD fame. The song was called "Boyz II

Men (The Sequel)", and actually featured the R&B group, Boyz II Men on the hook, which went:

"No one to guide me, I'm all alone…no one to cry on
I need shelter from the rain, to ease the pain
We're changing from boys to men"

The hook to this song played over and over in my head for some reason. The lyrics to that song stuck with me. It was that and the song that I played all throughout boot camp by Pete Rock & CL Smooth, "When They Reminisce Over You", on repeat in my head. To this day, those two songs hit different to me and will force me to lose it emotionally, every time.

One of the last conversations with my daddy Kenny, that stood out, was the one I had when I called him from the airport in Richmond. I was just about to catch a flight to El Paso for boot camp, and I called to let him know what I was doing. We talked for a little while, with me admitting to him that I was scared of going. In his typical fashion, he checked me and reminded me who I was and how he raised me to be, which was tough.

Remembering, this is the same guy who would arrange fights for me against almost every kid in the neighborhood, being scared is not an option. He also expressed how proud he was of me and that I was becoming a man. I seldomly would receive any type of approval from him like that, so it meant the world to me. That moment is one of the main memories I hold onto of my daddy Kenny. The pain and sorrow I was feeling is indescribable and my world felt completely crushed. After all of the things I had been going thru, I'm thinking what more could go wrong?

While roaming the hood in a daze, I ran into Pooh, who knew something was wrong with me. My eyes were red and swollen, with both fresh and dried-up tears running down my face. He, or anyone for that matter, had never seen me like this. I told him that my daddy had gotten killed and he invited me over to his house to hang out for the rest of the day. His mom is the sweetest. She basically consoled me and fixed us something to eat. I stayed at Pooh's house for the majority of the day. We ate, smoked, chilled, and watched Richard Pryor for some good laughs. I really appreciated him being there for me in that time of need. I'll never forget that.

I was required to spend that same summer going back to do additional military training, in which I did after heading to Florida to attend my daddy Kenny's funeral. The time I spent back in Polk County with my family, was eye-opening and put a lot of things into perspective for me. I had wasted a lot of time, making the worst decisions ever. I had so much more potential than this.

While down there, my Auntie Karen would push for me to go to college and really wanted me to go to Florida A&M University to pursue a degree in pharmacy. She was a RN and knew that the medical field would be a great career path. She knew of my passion for rap and would support me in that, but wanted me to do Christian rap instead, saying I could be the first one to make it popular and big. At the time, it was completely unheard of, but in hindsight, she was on to something.

I certainly didn't have college in the forefront of things that I wanted to do, as I only wanted to be a rapper. The reality, however, is that I didn't see any possible opportunity to make it happen at all. Given the headspace I was in at the moment, I wasn't sure about doing anything with my life. I felt so depressed and it showed by the continued activity of me getting into more and more trouble back in VA.

To me, my daddy Kenny, was a gangster n*gga. The first weed smoking, gun toting, bad a** I ever knew. People deal and react to losing a loved one, in different ways. My way of dealing with it was to try and embody everything that I felt my daddy Kenny was. Emulating the type of behavior that he was known for, would be my way of honoring my pops.

So, if you think I was trying to be hard before, it was on another level now. My attitude was "I don't care about nothing!" In the words of every gangsta rapper that I listened to from Cube, Snoop, Pac, to Face "I just don't give a f*ck!"

MISTER

Me and my sister, Kenya with Daddy Kenny

Kenneth Lamar Overstreet aka my "Daddy Kenny"

Buggin' Out

The National Guard made the mistake of having me do my additional training right there in my hometown of Petersburg, at Fort Lee, of all places. I had thugs coming on base to pull guns on some other soldiers I was beefing with in training, sneaking out of the barracks to hang out with the homies, and doing everything under the sun. I'm totally gone, getting high, drinking, and yet, coasting thru the training.

My stepdad happened to be a top commander right there on the base, so with any issues that I would run into involving any higher-ranking officials, I would just have him address it, to get me out of trouble. Miraculously, I ended up graduating from that training, the only thing I graduated from, and went straight back to the streets, getting involved in even more foolery.

College is officially out of the picture for me. I'm totally not interested. After not graduating and with my daddy Kenny passing away, along with the disappointment of nothing happening with any rap opportunities, you can miss me with all of that. To add more insult to injury, being that I'm wilding out and feeling myself, my girlfriend ended up breaking up with me and started dating a guy across town that I ended up having beef with. Why she do that?

I was trying to play it off, but I was having the heartbreak of my life, straight hurt, angry, and devastated. This would lead to more unnecessary fights and gunplay, surrounding the beef with this dude. The first time I ever saw a Tech Nine in person, was when this guy pointed one to my face. Those guns have a reputation for always jamming and divine intervention would make it so on that particular day.

This was such a turbulent time. I was so down and depressed, that I started experimenting with some of my mother's prescription pills and almost overdosed on 800mg Motrin. I remember just sitting in the lazy boy chair, just popping them back, like "I wonder what will happen if I just keep taking these?" I took two at first, then another one, and another one, another one, until I passed out. Long story short, I ended up in the back of an ambulance and by the grace of God, I made it thru. You would think after that, I would come back to my senses, but nope!

After going thru that scare, I really started *Buggin Out*. I ended up catching a case for assaulting a police officer with a Louisville Slugger. I had no idea he was a cop. I just thought he was some obnoxious, white guy that was sticking his business somewhere it didn't belong. He had on plain clothes, so how was I supposed to know he was an officer of the law? Given the environment, I used to go everywhere with that bat and he happened to catch the opposite end of the handle on that day.

I went to jail and my parents had to come get me out. I felt so bad for them. They were doing the best job ever in making sure I had everything that I needed and wanted, most of the time. Yet, here I am, trying to break every law under the sun, being the rebellious teenager that I was. I had completely lost all focus. All of this 'hanging' had reached the point to where it wasn't safe to go anywhere.

There were guys popping up at my house to fight, calling my house and threatening to shoot up the crib. One night I remember a shot blast actually coming thru my living room window, while I was watching television. Like, I'm at the point now where my life is really in jeopardy and my family is wrapped up in it as well. It was a must to roll everywhere deep, with a bunch of guys that were ready for anything at any moment. It didn't matter if you were just going to the mall, the movies, a restaurant, or even church. The drama was everywhere.

One night I was caught slipping in the wrong part of town, which resulted in me being completely outnumbered, getting jumped, pistol whipped, and chased out, literally, by gunfire. I had the pedal to the metal in my little white Geo Metro, running every red light, and praying for police to appear, which they didn't. Any other time, you can't go anywhere without them all in the way. Now, all of a sudden, when the heat is on, they ain't nowhere in sight. Luckily, by the grace of God, I made it out of that alive.

Maybe that would bring me back to my senses, but nope! We would go thru this type of stuff, make it out, then plot on ways for get back. We would even tell the stories and laugh about it, like right after it happened, with heart pumping, and all. The way we were living our lives was pure insanity. My only excuse was that I was just hurt and depressed, to the point where nothing mattered much to me anyway.

My life was to the point where my everyday was ducking enemies to having police pull us over with guns drawn, just for driving. To cope, we would get together, roll dice at the bus stops, hang out, drinking 40 ounces of malt liquor, smoking weed, and sniffing coke.

Yep, I had turned to substance abuse heavy during this time. Thru Mike, who in the streets was known by Krook, I was introduced to a lot of real gangsters, that took a liking to me enough to hang, but trust me, when Real gangster activity was going down, they wouldn't allow me to have no parts of it.

One of the main hangouts was a spot called "Da Run", which was short for Bermuda Run. This area was infamous for having every element of crime you can think of. It was only one way in and out of this huge complex. It's where you could go to find a few bad chicks, drugs, guns, and trouble. I bought my first gun, a .22 caliber revolver, in Da Run.

With all its drama, it wasn't all that bad. You could have fun there too, but you not stepping foot in there without a cosign from one of the big homies. You definitely needed to know somebody there. It was our own little version of the infamous Queensbridge projects, that we used to hear about thru Nas and Mobb Deep's music. Overall, it was unassumingly dangerous, but it was one of our stomping grounds.

Somewhere around that time, I had got the nickname of "Skate". So, to most of the homies out there in the hood, that's what I was known by. I guess they'll be damned if they call me "Mister."

"that's Skate from Ft. Lee, ran with Pooh, Greg, and them Hung wit Lil Larry from JC, hooked up with Krook and Ronski

My man Pete set it off, better have a gun if it's Big E" – MR Nasty

It's to the point, where I'm hanging out in the projects damn near every day, with the homies, even if it was just to chill and play video games or kick rhymes for entertainment. Yet, in the middle of all that, it was always a war going on.

Allen Iverson aka Bubbachuck, who's also from Virginia, Bad News, to be exact, is known for having a tattoo on his arm that reads "Cru-Thik." I totally could relate to that, because in VA, that's exactly how we were made and rolled out. I can't even begin to name a fraction of the crew that I hung with, but there was click of them who you can find me kicking it with on numerous occasions.

There was a line that Nas said once, that went "*there ain't no drama that my n*ggaz never handled for me.*" I can relate to that also, because these guys were all known to get Active and was what you had coming, if there ever was an issue. Some of these guys are serving life sentences, some served lengthy sentences and made it home, and a few, unfortunately, have passed away, and there's a good amount of them that made it thru the struggle and are out, alive, well and have transitioned to bosses in their respective areas in life.

You had your knock-out artists like E-Bo and Damon, hustlers like Cool V, Gus, Ferg, Lil Larry, and Diggs (rip), straight gangsters like Krook, Ski aka Gimme, and Lonski, guys quick to set it off, like Pete and Wildman, hitters like Gio, Rog McBride (rip), Pooh, Spanky, Reggie Gregory, and the craziest individuals in the likes of Shawn Love, Big J (rip), lil Greg, Rob, Will and Larry Anderson, and James Ferg.

There's a story of some famous gangsters from London called Reggie and Ronnie Kray. I got a kick out of that, once I read up about them, because I was also raised with two wild brothers by the name of Reggie and Ronnie Hicks.

You even had the younger homies, who were just as ruthless, like JJ Shaw, Dre, Elwyn, Cody, Lil Leon, Sheed, Louie, Meat, Midnite, Sup, and Julius, who some of them played ball, but all of them were kicking it heavy and catching all fades across town.

Catch us rolling ten to fifteen-deep everywhere, hopping off the back of a truck, or jumping out cars, with bats, brass knuckles, knives, guns, tasers, with razors under the tongue. We wearing Timberland boots year-round, Nike flavas, and New Balance sneakers, rocking Starter jackets inside out, with LA Raiders or LA Kings ball caps on, croaker sack pullovers, sweatshirts, champion hoodies, or donned out in Carhartt with Dickie pants.

We all had sky pagers and if we was really getting money, you had the brick phone to go with it, along with the herringbone or link chain, to match. Every sinister laugh showcased the gold fronts in the mouth, with the nappy twists or fade with the 360 waves.

The personalities of everybody was so twisted, you could be chilling and smoking with somebody that afternoon and he'll show up later that evening with a gang of dudes from another side of town, gun in hand, on some "wassup!" It was hard to tell who was really your friend or who was plotting to get you on any given day of the week. You never knew who or when you could be "food", so you had to keep your head on a swivel and stay low key.

All of the mind games, questionable characters, and uncertainty of the day is enough to drive someone insane. On top of that, you gotta watch out for these crazy chicks that will set you up in a heartbeat. It seemed like the best-looking girls that was really interested in you, always seem to live in the neighborhoods where you ain't welcomed. So now you gotta roll four to five deep just to pay her a visit and sneak in and out of her hood. I literally got caught just outside of a girl's window once and was glad it was the cops that caught me instead of the dudes that lived there.

This is what you get, when you mix a group of have and have not teens, throw them in a small town, just outside the murder capitol, with no real opportunities, and add in Boredom! It's all the right ingredients for a powder keg.

I recall partying out in Richmond with the gang and getting into it with a couple of guys inside the party. These same guys ended up being gunned down right in front of me just outside on the block. The gunshots were so close range, that it literally looked like the shooter was stabbing the guy with the gun. It was two shooters busting their guns in unison, so the shots rang out like fireworks, with smoke to go along with it. "Blatt, blatt, blat, blat, blat, blat, blat…" I was in complete shock watching it, as I was standing right there and saw a girl get shot that was nearby as well.

After gunning down the victims, the shooters turned their guns toward my way. Bystanders are nothing more than expendable eyewitnesses, so it

MISTER

was no thrill running for my life, while dodging bullets hailed in my direction. By the time I made it to my car, where a drunk and awakened Pooh was, the shooting subsided and I did my best to maneuver a stick shift vehicle, weaving thru traffic in downtown Richmond. Pooh was strapped, so he pulled out and was anxious to bust his gun in any direction of opposition.

After clearing the scene, I remember we left the rest of the homies inside the club, so we circled back to pick up the rest of the crew, and arrived to see yellow tape, a stunned crowd, and police everywhere. Needless to say, we all got a kick out of the entire events of the night, driving back to Petersburg, bumping some Onyx, while getting high. I made it home that night, totally shook up, with my parents asking me if I had fun at the skating rink. I assured them that I had fun, but all the while running thru my high mind, was me running from bullets and watching two kids get murdered. Two kids that could have easily been three.

This was just another day in VA, nothing out of the norm at all, but for me, sobering. Just to think, I asked for all of this madness. Please believe, I had friends, like Al, who wasn't going thru this at all. As crazy as this may sound, the times, as dangerous as they were, was some of the most fun and exciting times of my life. Kind of sad, but true.

What exactly am I doing with my life? All I really want to do is just rap and be somebody. This can't be it. My life seemed to be spiraling out of control and I was seeking a lifeline fast.

In between, fights, shootouts, and run ins with the law, the group would eventually fall stagnant and really missed opportunities to really make something happen with it. Krook was the driving force behind getting us the most attention when it came to the rap, so without his focus and availability, due to him being too much in the thick of things, there weren't many options.

Another thing, this isn't New York City or Los Angeles, we lived in Virginia, what the hell else is there to do but get into trouble?! It ain't like we had a studio every four blocks or something. There was no school of the arts or neighbor that had an album out, putting everybody on. We had to know people with those types of connections and we never made it out of Virginia to go other places and find out how to go about getting on. We only knew to just rap, and our ceiling had us really content with just being hood celebrities.

With the mindset I had at the time, being a hood celebrity known for rapping or thuggin was fine with me. I was on a path headed to nowhere and really didn't care. My father had just passed away, I was still dealing with a heartbreak, I lost my scholarships, my parents had given up on me in my eyes and who could blame them. Hell, even my sister, Kenya, was out in the streets wilding out just as much, if not, more than I was. She was also taking the loss of daddy Kenny pretty hard. My parents ended up sending her back to Florida to live with our grandmother.

I mean, it is what it is. Such is life and we just trying to live it and figure it out as we go. Meanwhile, I'm literally the guy that's walking around now, with gun in the waist, hiding it in my shoebox at home, attracting different chicks around town, because that's one of the perks of being a "thug." With nothing else more exciting to do, I'm still hanging out in hoods with killers and drug dealers, getting high off coke and weed. I'm so not cut from the cloth of the circle I was so closely knit to, yet I felt a part of something big.

The more rap wasn't happening for me, the more I settled for the allure of the streets. Looking back, I had to be the most smartest, stupidest, dumbest, nerd n*gga alive. The scary part of that is, I really meant it and was on that type of time. All it would have taken, was me being put in more positions to test where I stood, situations to prove how much I'm really about pulling that trigger, robbing that cab driver, running up in that bank, or moving that pack, pressuring me to make the dumbest decisions ever, all just to impress the gang. Choices that could have changed the trajectory of my entire life. Choices that so many of my close friends would actually make, leading to life and death consequences.

Thank God for a praying mother, is all I can say. In the meantime, though, "we ouchea, Thug Life, we living it baby!" This is usually when the tragic wakeup call is inevitable. However, my wakeup call came in a very different, safe, and exciting form. It came in the form of Love.

The Love

Larry had a neighbor that he was "seeing" at the time, who was originally from Queens, New York. One day her cousin came in town from Queens to visit and we clicked instantly. This girl swept me off of my feet. Everything from her style of dress and the way that she talked, had me head over heels. Not only that, she was absolutely gorgeous and I was ready to settle down on the day that I met her.

We kicked it during her entire visit down in VA. She was so in tune with me and it seemed like she hung onto every word I would say. I would scoop her up and she would ride out with me around the city, while listening to A Tribe Called Quest, who she was very familiar with, being they were from the same place. She was my encyclopedia for all things New York related and would answer all the questions I had about this mecca of hip hop. It wasn't long before she had to go back home and we remained in touch. We then got involved in a long-distance relationship, that led me heading to NYC for my first time ever in life to visit her.

This trip to Queens would be the icing on the cake for me, the wakeup call I wasn't expecting. While in NY, I had a chance to experience almost everything the city had to offer. I ate some New York pizza, went to Jamaica Ave and got my first gold fronts at the Coliseum. The highlight was when we took the dollar van to the Nu-Clear cleaners at Linden Blvd. Anybody that know me, knows how much I love Tribe and this is where they shot the infamous video for "Check the Rhime". I was in complete awe and didn't want to leave. Everything about this trip was heaven to me. I loved the air, the buildings, the fact that everyone was in a hurry, the fast talk, the noise, the leather jackets, the bridges, the subways, everything just screamed Hip Hop!!

I could easily see how living in this city would drive anyone to want to be an emcee. I wish I could have stayed there and not gone back home at all. I credit this girl for getting my focus back. We would have long talks and she would encourage me to turn things around and be the person that I really am. She saw the compassionate, soft hearted, and smart individual that I truly was and would beg me to stop the thug foolishness. That kind of stuff she witnessed all of the time in New York. It was definitely something to not glorify and an element she longed to get away from. She couldn't wait to get out of New York. Me, on the other hand, wanted all of it!

Our relationship would eventually end due to long distance and us not having the means to constantly see each other. We stayed in touch and remained close friends, with her constantly reminding me of how dope I was with rhyming and to not give up.

I was back in VA, with a battery in my back and a renewed energy of wanting to make something happen with this rap game. Of course, the streets and all of the bs that came with it was still there, but I was more focused on staying away from it. Every experience became a verse or a song, which I found it to be very therapeutic. I have notebooks, scratch papers, napkins, all of which are all full of verses that can tell my whole life story.

One of my most prolific songs, describing the most recent events at the moment, was called "1993...Lest I Forget." It was a record that I wrote, but never truly recorded. I did a reference to it sometime later, but never released. I would perform it for a few friends and even my parents, at one point, but never solicited it. It was really something written for me to cope with all of the negativity that came about during the year and helped me to heal a little bit. Whenever I was going thru anything, I would turn to some song to match my emotions at the time, as a way for me to get thru.

You see, since our first introduction, hip-hop has been the only constant throughout my whole life thus far. *The Love* I had for hip-hop was growing stronger by the minute. It became a part of everything I did and wanted to do. After going through so many let-downs in my life at this point, I was really searching to gain some sort of meaning for my life. I did everything my parents, elders, or counselors told me to do that they thought was best for my future. I mean, all the way down to joining the military.

My bad decisions and rebellious nature had me getting kicked out of both school and the military eventually. I would work from one job to the next, entertaining coworkers with rhymes and getting nothing but compliments, like "mane, you should be on."

I would get home and watch videos on MTV and BET, thinking that I could be on there too. I know I'm good enough and I have people everywhere, from school, the church, and even the hood, telling me that I have what it takes. I was convinced, as well, that I had the talent to make it, but how?? I eventually came to the conclusion that nothing, and I mean

MISTER

NOTHING would quench my thirst of success than that of making it into the rap industry.

My parents, of course, didn't agree with me wanting to make 'devil' music as a career. They would always say that it's not of the Lord, first of all, and that it is a dream that could not happen. "You need to prepare for your future first son, go to college, get a good job…then do your rap thing if you want to. That way you have something to fall back on." I would grow to hate and constantly be haunted by that phrase. Though I love them to death, my parents were my first "haters."

That led to my motivation to prove them and whoever else wrong. I vowed to make this 'dream' become a 'reality'. I vowed to make it onto that STAGE, onto that TV SCREEN, onto that ALBUM, and onto whatever else that came with it! Though I hadn't the slightest clue of where to start or 'know how' of going about it, THIS became my passion…to make it on the Inside!

Mr. Muhammad

So here it is, 1994…I'm still in Petersburg, Virginia, getting in all types of trouble. I had just got kicked out of school the year before and lost all my scholarships for college. My parents were trying to get me to go to school in Florida when they moved back. Apparently, the amount of trouble I had gotten into and issues I caused for my dad on Fort Lee, was too much for them at this point, and it was time to go.

I refused to leave and bounced from house to house, living here to there, with my best friend, Larry and his parents in Petersburg one minute, then in Hampton with my other homie, Al who had just joined the Air Force, stationed at Langley. I was at the point where I'd squandered all of my academic opportunities and really wasn't interested anyway. Some way or another, I had to figure out how to get into "a" music scene.

No one that I was around had any clue on how to go about it. So, I was left to just dream and entertain friends with verses from time to time. All the while, hanging out, chasing girls and money, and trying to stay alive in the midst of drama. I was with the homies hitting up every town to just kick it, all up and down I-64, from the Tidewater area to Richmond.

As chance would have it, one night we stumbled upon a venue in Richmond that just so happened to be hosting an open mic showcase downtown at the 6th street market. Larry and Al had gone with me and hyped me up to rhyme. I ended up being the first one to spit. The host that night

MISTER

was a DJ by the name of Mad Skillz. Oh yea, he rhymed too! Anyway, he had me stand on this chair in the middle of the club and told me to go. I don't even know what beat I had or verse I kicked, all I know is my homies said that I killed it and the crowd was feeling me. That was the first time I ever rhymed in front of a crowd…unless you count the times in the school cafeteria or in the projects rhyming in a crack spot full of dope dealers and gangsters. Other than that, I had popped my cherry that night and will never forget that first experience. Rocking the mic, is Definitely something I could get used to.

A little while later, I came up on tickets to see De La Soul and A Tribe Called Quest at a show they had at the Hampton Coliseum. Yes, the same group whose tape was the first I owned, "3 Feet High and Rising", was performing and I was able to attend. On top of that, as you know by now, I am a Tribe fanatic!

On this particular night, I was with my cousin, Eric, who somehow escaped the Bucket of Polk County, Florida and moved in with his Aunt, who lived off of Big Bethel Rd. in Hampton. He rode out with me and Al. Anyway, for the entire show I was just mesmerized…just staring at these dudes in amazement like, Wow, it's really them!

These guys were like gods to me. Q-Tip had this effortless charisma about him that enabled him to command the stage with ease. Phife Dawg delivered such rawness and attitude with his rhyme flow that I really gravitated to. Besides that, I related to him, being that we were similar in height and dark skinned. Watching him, was like looking at myself up there on the stage. On the Ones and Twos was *Mr. Muhammad* himself, providing the soundboard for a show that I would remember for a lifetime.

They ripped everything off the Midnight Marauders album that had just come out and the earlier classics like "<u>Can I Kick It</u>" and "<u>Check The Rhime</u>". De La killed it too with the joints from the Buhloone Mindstate album they had just dropped. All of a sudden, at the end of the show, they decided to have an impromptu freestyle session, which I loved to watch. I couldn't really freestyle back then.

I remember when Mike, tried to teach me how to freestyle, both him and Pooh. It was crazy…Mike was like, "when you get stuck, just scream aaahhh!" As funny as that may sound, I tried it, and it worked:

> **"I'm ridin down da block, lookin for da cops**
> **Finger on da Glock, when I see em I'ma –aaaahhh**
> **Shoot em den I'm out, out, yea aahh watch out…"**

Soon, there were less "aaahhhs" and more words that rhymed, practice is the key, as I would find out. Back to the concert, the freestyle session was on and they brought out a special guest. A skinny cat, with dreadlocks came out on stage and immediately I'm looking at this cat like "I know him". It was Mad Skillz from Richmond, VA. I'm tripping like I just seen this dude! After the show, I loitered around the barricade by the backstage, obviously not wanting this moment to end. As I stared at Ali Shaheed Muhammad taking his equipment down, I noticed Mad Skillz. I called him over to me and he came by the barricade. My cousin, already knowing what time it was, started yelling for Mr. Muhammad, like "come here." By this time, I'm trying to get Mad Skillz to remember me. I'm like, "hey, you remember me from the showcase in Richmond, "my name Mister?" He was like, "yea, I put you on first." He then said like the first two bars of my rhyme, no lie.

My cousin's attempt worked too, Ali came over and my cousin started bragging on me, "hey man, my cuz can rap, put him on." It was at that point where Ali gave me the contact for his label, Jive Records. He told me to call them and send them my demo. I was so hyped yo! It was crazy. I'm here chopping it up with Mad Skillz and Ali Shaheed Muhammad; this guy remembered my rhyme and the DJ from A Tribe Called Quest just gave me the contact for a major label…crazy, if you from VA then you know…this just doesn't happen everyday man.

This was my breakthrough, my first encounter of experiencing a close contact with someone actually inside the industry. Back to the matter at hand…with information for the label on Varick Street in New York City, and a renowned rapper from my hometown remembering me, I went back to doing…nothing!

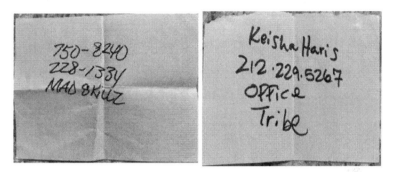

Contact that I got from Mad Skillz at the show.

Contact info from Ali Shaheed Muhammad

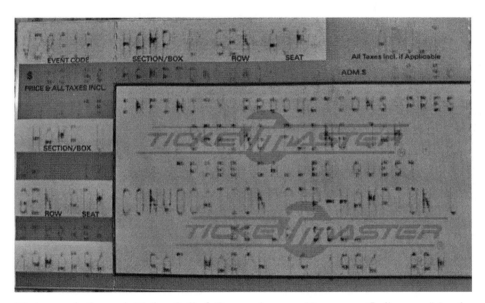

Ticket stub from A Tribe Called Quest show at Hampton Coliseum, March 19, 1994

Excursions

I remained in between Petersburg and Hampton, trapped by the same dead-end elements that I vowed to escape from. Though I was still writing raps like crazy and killing ciphers everywhere, from church to the hood, I had no knowledge of how to record a demo or find anybody with a studio.

So, there I was, doing nothing with my life, engaging in all types of unhealthy and dead-end *Excursions*, until I spoke with a homeboy who had just moved down to Atlanta and put us onto our best excursion yet.

My homie Ralph, was Mike's cousin, who was from around the way and used to make beats back in High School. He used to get down with some dudes from the other side that went to our school, so we didn't really do any music together then. However, he and his group were performing at the school basketball games and had a plug on recording as well. He seemed to be making a little more headway in that area, but again, he was doing all of that with those other guys that we didn't really rock with at the time.

Ralph used to stay out in Jackson Circle with Mike and Larry. He was a very quiet guy, that kept to himself mostly and played basketball. Very early on, Ralph had a car and was a girl magnet, making moves on his own. I remember when he used to come over to Larry's house with his Alesis drum machine and play some beats he made. They were good, but we never hung out much to actually make a connection. Anyway, his mom moved him down to Atlanta after he got kicked out of the same school for selling drugs. It seems that our whole crew got kicked out of school at some point.

So, all the while, I'm in VA living "la vida loca", he was down in the "A" soaking in the musical renaissance that was forming…fast! I don't know who called who, but I remember him saying, "Yo, you need to come down here to Atlanta for Freaknik". I'm thinking, "what the hell is a Freaknik". Al was like, "let's just drive down there". We drove about 8 ½ hours down to Atlanta, hitting Hwy 58 from Hampton, to I-95, to I-26, to I-20. Man, soon as we got to Colombia, SC it was bananas.

We found ourselves in a parade of cars headed the same way and everybody was wilding out on the road and everything. I'm talking about people standing up thru the sunroof of their cars, blasting music. Girls were topless, hanging out the window, with drinks flowing. Mind you, we hadn't even hit the Georgia state line and it was jumping! I got a speeding ticket and everything, leading to my license getting suspended, but hey, blame it on Freaknik '94 baby!

Once we got to Atlanta, it was stupid…traffic was in gridlock the whole weekend. We met up with Ralph in College Park and we went to where he stayed with his mom off of Camp Creek Pkwy in an apartment called Pine Crossings at the time. The theme music for the weekend was, of course, a Tribe Called Quest, Wutang Clan, Snoop Doggy Dogg, and this new album from an artist named Nas called "Illmatic".

I can't even explain all the events that went down and the celebrity faces we spotted all over the city. Being a guy from a small town in VA, this experience was…drugs! Anybody that went to Freaknik '94 or '95 know what time it is, so I don't have to describe the craziness that goes down at

MISTER

Freaknik. If you're too young to know what I'm talking about, ask your parents, uncle, or favorite auntie about it. I'm positive they can tell you stories. The great thing about the entire experience, is that the city of Atlanta was so electrifying, AND it was full of black people…with money!

It was during this time, that Ralph and I really made a connection. He was playing a lot of his beats that he made in the car and I would just rhyme to them all day. Ralph had made a few connections in Atlanta, having gone to school with Usher Raymond and hung out with him and his friends, he was in an industry circle already.

I remember linking with one of his homegirls that took us to Too Short's house off of Cascade Rd. He had the huge swimming pool in the back yard that had his dollar sign logo in the middle of it. His mother was there, very hospitable lady that went thru pictures in the photo album with us. I'm looking at candid photos of Too Short, hanging out with Eazy E, I mean, it was crazy.

It was cool to notice all of the spots that were being made famous by Outkast, which was the new group out of the city. Places like East Point, College Park where Ralph lived, the Underground, and Greenbriar were already becoming household names. This leads to the next 'inside' moment.

As irony would have it, while stuck in traffic, we were listening to the radio and they said that Outkast was shooting their video at a spot called Capone's on Peachtree. We stopped and asked a random stranger where it was and we were out. I was kind of excited to get a chance to see these dudes. All I knew of them was that song they had just put out called "Players Ball."

The video was sick, and it was kind of weird seeing guys from down south spitting like that, lyrical and everything.

Back to the scene…we pull up and the camera crews are out, people walking around everywhere…they were shooting the scene in the alleyway, inside the car smoking. I caught a glimpse of them in the ride and was trying to be extra nosey, but they kept everybody away. At this point, it's me, Al, and Ralph. We decided to just go inside the spot. Once we get in, the first person I see is Big Boi at the bar talking to some chick. Andre, who wasn't 3000 at the time, came in and asked Big Boi to borrow $5 real quick for something. I'm not sure as to why I specifically remember that. Maybe, it was the southern accent in the way he said it that stuck out. This was the same southern twang that they both maintained in their music. It was very different, new, and gravitating.

I was also tripping to see them with almost the same outfits from the first video. I guess so you could remember who they were and it worked because I spotted them immediately. Moving along, we stayed close to the bar, of course, and in walks this little dude that looked very familiar…it was Jermaine Dupri, and right behind him was Kris Kross and this fine, light skinned chick with them.

They all had on shirts that read, "So So Def" in a crazy, huge font. They posted up by the wall at the bar where we were. I'm so celebrity shocked, but far from shy, I didn't know what to do with myself. I go over to Kris Kross and introduce myself to them. They were real cool and all I was thinking was, "damn, these is them 'jump jump' dudes man". C'mon now, y'all know y'all was digging Kris Kross…don't hate on the Totally Krossed Out movement.

After speaking to them, I went over to the girl that was with them and immediately went into 'game mode'. I told her my name and asked, "what's your name"; she said "my name Brat". Not knowing anything at this point, I'm like "Brat?…what you do Brat, you rap or something?" She said, "yea, a little bit". I pour it on now; I tell her "me and my man right here do music too…we got some music coming out soon". She's like, "oh word, that's wassup".

I guess he finally got tired of me 'playing myself', because Ralph then gets in my ear and he's like, "yo, that's Da Brat…the girl who did that verse on Da Bomb". I can't even remember what happened after that, except me feeling stupid. She then yelled out "wassup Ceelo". It was Ceelo Green from Goodie Mob, but of course I had no clue of who he or they were at the time. I then noticed faces that turned out to be the likes of Big Rube, Rico Wade, Bigg Gipp, and a new director to the industry, F. Gary Gray.

On that note, F. Gary Gray called everybody to the floor to shoot the next part of the video. Are you serious? Are we about to be in a video?!! What?! Yes, people, my first video shoot experience…long hours and a million takes for "Southernplayalisticadillacmuzik" by Outkast!

When it came out, me and Al was showing everybody back home in VA our cameo. Even though we had to stand next to the TV and point ourselves out every time, you couldn't tell us nothing, we were famous!! As a side bar, I'd like to point out that Ralph got cussed out by his mom, because we didn't make it back home until daybreak. To explain how serious it was, me and Al snuck out the crib and hit the highway, all the way back to VA…still high off the whole Freaknik '94 weekend!

Find A Way

I remember thinking to myself when I got back to VA that I've got to *Find A Way* to Atlanta, first chance I get! I definitely saw it as the place where I could make the most of an opportunity to get Inside. It also helped that a close friend of mine, Ralph, was connected. Al agreed! Everything felt good, things were moving in the right direction.

Shortly after, we went to Norfolk to catch A Tribe Called Quest, again, with Large Professor, who was part of a major rap group called Main Source. Large Professor was also credited with helping to launch Nas' career.

The city was crazy that night, streets was packed. For some reason, we got there too late and weren't able to get in because it was filled to capacity inside the venue. Luckily, the spot was all glass so you could watch the performance from the outside. I was struck again…watching Large Professor and Tribe side by side on stage. I saw Mad Skillz again that night too. This time it was on some quick "waddup" and he was out. We were in Norfolk, not the type of town to just meander around.

Watching the show through the glass, gave me another memorable feeling. It was like something out of a movie. I was on the outside looking in, thinking to myself that "I'm gonna make it inside the glass one day, to know what it's like."

To escape some of the madness going on in VA, I decided to head down to Florida to visit family for a little bit and ended up staying with my stepmother, in the house where my daddy Kenny had lived. I was just really missing him and wanted to be in touch with something familiar. I took the time to gather my thoughts and stay focused.

While I was there, my stepmother introduced me to a friend of hers that was a musician in the area. He was a singer that performed at local gigs. After an evening at his house, showing him that I knew how to play the trumpet he had, he and a partner of his took a liking to me. My stepmother told them that I could also rap, so I kicked a few rhymes for them, and they were very impressed.

They asked if I would be cool with performing at a venue in Tampa, Florida. Mind you, I had never done a show anywhere, outside of just rhyming at the open mic in Richmond earlier. To actually have a performance slot at a venue, was a totally different ball game.

I didn't have any original songs to perform, so I decided to write something specifically for the show. I also didn't have any original tracks, so I went the route of using the instrumental that was on the flip side of an Outkast single I had for Player's Ball. On both sides, it had instrumentals for both versions of the record. I planned to perform two songs and use both instrumentals to rock over.

I practiced for hours at the house, using an imaginary microphone, while speaking to an imaginary crowd of people, telling them to put their hands in the air. I really wanted my performance to come off right. Besides, this would be my very first time and I wanted to impress the gentleman who gave me this shot.

MISTER

I tried hard to think about something I could say for crowd participation and I recalled a performance I saw recently by 2pac on MTV JAMS. During his show, he was performing his hit single, "I Get Around" and during the hook, he would yell "aint no party like a thug life party, cuz a thug life party don't stop." He would repeat it over and over, having the crowd in a frenzy.

I decided to use the same chant but switched the words to reflect me being in Tampa Bay, by saying "aint no party like a bay side party, cuz a bay side party don't stop." To add on the end of that, I pulled a chant from another artist. Doug E. Fresh had a song out called "A-yo, Aiight." The hook was basically just a crowd participation winner, by having everyone say "AaaaaaaYooooo...Aaaiigghht!" I snatched that and added that piece at the end of the other 2Pac hook. I prepared two verses, with that hook in between. I definitely learned early that preparation is key.

The show went off like a charm. I was totally surprised by the response I received from the crowd and I had the place rocking! I can't describe the feeling of being on the stage at that club, doing what I love, and the people were enjoying it. I was unknown to them, but the energy had them in it. It felt good to not disappoint the guys who gave me the opportunity and I'm forever grateful for it.

This was added ammunition to keep pushing. I just couldn't believe that my first stage show opportunity came about in Polk County, Florida, of all places. Not long after, I had received a letter from Ralph. It was basically a motivation letter, encouraging me to keep at it and to trust him that we had what it takes to make this music thing happen. He and I were both still hype off of our connection during Freaknik and knew we had a common goal to get Inside.

With the letter, he had sent me a tape of beats to write to and said that he was arranging for us to be able to get a demo put together. I was extremely excited about that! This was all we needed to get us to the next step. Afterall, I still hadn't sent a demo over to Ali Shaheed Muhammad and needed desperately to do so before it was too late. Things were moving at a snail's pace, but it was progress nonetheless.

So, during the summer of '94, while everybody was trying to figure out if O.J. did it or not, me and Ralph was recording our first demo in Richmond at my man Travis spot, off Hull Street. Even though I started out rhyming with Mike, Pooh, and Larry, I connected with Ralph on another level. We seem to have a good chemistry when it came to our collaborations.

At a young age, Ralph was a genius to me with the music. His dad, who died when he was like two or three years old, was a jazz musician, so it was in his blood. He always had some crazy ideas for songs and I thrive on going 'left', so we clicked instantly. I say all that to say…we had an objective…to get INSIDE.

We completed the demo and it turned out pretty good. A couple of the records we did, came off very good, with me and Ralph complimenting each other well. One of the favorites to stand out was "Word Is Real" and another song, called "So What". These would be the two songs that we would end up performing often. If you wanna know what it kind of sounded like, I would say A Tribe Called Quest (but of course) meets Digable Planets.

MISTER

It was such a feeling of accomplishment after we finished it. I had been waiting so long just to pass this obstacle, that was holding me back from so many opportunities. So now I have a demo and I'm ready to send it off to Jive Records with the info I got from Ali Shaheed Muhammad. We mailed off the demo and I spent days, weeks, months, of speaking to a secretary and no acknowledgment of anyone receiving the demo and/or listening to it. I was definitely disappointed and didn't understand why he would mislead me and have the office jerk me around like that.

Time was dragging out and I was still involved in heavy beef with ignorant, jealous, and bored individuals from cross-town. I needed something to happen, fast! Even though I got kicked out of school, I was able to test out and received my Advanced High School diploma, with honors, in the mail.

After which, Virginia State University, actually offered me a grant for one semester to attend. I was excited about it and toured the campus, but quickly realized, that if I stayed in Virginia, I would still be dealing with the same street drama that I could not seem to escape at the time. Besides that, I didn't have any luck with finding any musical connections to make anything happen.

My music partner, Ralph, was in Atlanta and his mother had him super focused on finishing school. I had no other big ideas, so by default, I settled for the 'plan B'. With my Auntie Karen, who was urging me to pursue a degree in Pharmacy, my mom finally convinced me to go to college down in Florida. I used my grandmother's address to get in-state tuition and my parents took out loans to get me in at another HBCU, Florida A&M University.

If you recall, I had made the decision to join the National Guard back when I was a Junior in High School. When I joined, I was promised that I would receive a couple thousands of dollars as a bonus, but in addition, the Army was supposed to pay for my school tuition in the form of a grant, GI Bill, and loan repayment that covered up to $25,000 for school. They did give me the $2500 bonus, after combing thru the fine print, I discovered the loan repayment would take effect after serving eight years, the GI Bill was only $140 monthly, which barely covered my books, and the state of Virginia stopped awarding tuition assistance grants for National Guard. In other words, I was bamboozled.

I took the liberty of writing a letter to my commander, expressing my grievance, explaining the whole purpose of me joining the military was to pay for my education, if that wasn't happening, then I wanted out. I wasn't receiving any correspondence about resolving the issue, so I did exactly what any rebellious, non-authority liking, teenager would do. I went AWOL. I refused to go back and put on another uniform. I knew the consequences of my actions, but I didn't care. I felt I did everything that I was supposed to do, so…catch me if you can!

I guess I should add that, all of this with me signing up for the Army, wouldn't have been necessary had I not been kicked out of school for fighting and lost all of my academic scholarships. Nevertheless…I hit the highway and headed to Tallahassee, Florida.

MISTER

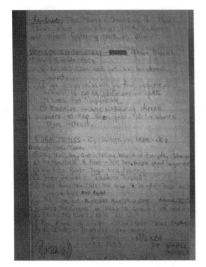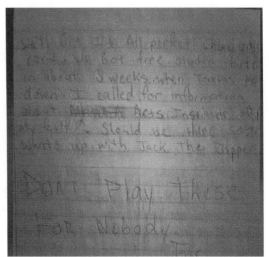

Letter from Ralph talking about studio time to record demo

With Raphael aka R Dot Fisher - SALAAM

Lyrics to Go

"F.A.M.U"

It didn't take long for me to get into the music scene down at FAMU. You have to remember, this is 1994, and Hip Hop was still on the incline heavy. For instance, some of the albums that came out that year were Illmatic, Southernplayalisticcadillacmuzik, Above the Rim soundtrack, Ready to Die, Tical, Dare Iz A Darkside, Murder Was the Case, Resurrection, Funkdafied, Most Beautifullest Thing In This World, etc....to name a few.

This was also still the era of "the cipher". Anybody who was somebody known for rhyming on campus, was somebody because they were known to BODY "the cipher". Needless to say, I've been involved in more ciphers than I can ever remember, but the ones I had at FAMU were monumental.

The very FIRST night on campus, a cipher broke out with about six to seven guys. We were all going for ours and even came up with a hook in between turns, "cuz ima pimp b*tch". Rhyme after rhyme after rhyme, all night, all day, anywhere, everywhere, didn't matter. All you would see were different packs of students, huddled up, with heads bopping.

Out of one of those ciphers, I caught the attention of a local promoter who hooked it up for me to open for Outkast at the largest venue in the city, Club Moon. Once it was confirmed that I was getting the opportunity to do the show, I called my partner Ralph up. He was four hours away in Atlanta, so I knew he would probably want to come down for this. He was on the next Greyhound smoking to Tallahassee.

We practiced for hours in my dorm room. We had this show intro that my man Travis from Richmond had made for us. Travis had the studio where, me and Ralph recorded our first demo under the group name, Salaam. The intro was bass heavy and had a sample of Travis saying "salaam, salaam, salaam" in different pitches. It was hard as hell yo! We figured that we would come out and freestyle over that for like eight bars apiece, then get into the set.

The show was good…practice pays off! We got a chance to chill in the VIP with Outkast after that, but that was quickly terminated once they got into it with another group that was on the ticket that night…a group called Gangsta Shorties from Miami. These dudes somehow tried Andre on some "yall ain't no better than us" type of vibe and he hopped up and called for Big Boi who I was just talking to at the time (well, not really-I spoke, he spoke back). That's when I saw their unity within the group and how you have to be out on the road in these different towns, having to watch your back from multiple haters. Either way, it was the second time popping my head on the INSIDE.

It wasn't long after that, the same promoter…wait a minute…let me take the time to acknowledge the guys that made the show happen. Shout out to Chocolate from Elizabeth City, NJ and my man Walt G. These guys saw potential in my talent very early on and decided to support, which is huge. After the success of the Club Moon show, these same gentleman worked it out for us to open up for the Lady of Rage on a brief 3-city tour that hit Tallahassee, Jacksonville, and Tampa.

We were both hyped about this one, because the Lady of Rage was from VA, so we had something to talk about…which we made sure we did backstage. Rage was super cool and sweeter than her persona of being "ruff and stuff". The real "ruff" one was her manager, Mrs. Sharitha Knight aka Mrs. Suge Knight. She was very "bitchy" and was on Rage's every move, looking over her shoulder. She was being all rude to the fans, telling Rage "that's enough autograph signing, let's go." It was interesting to hear people like Snoop Dogg, Rage, and Dogg Pound talk about how they weren't particularly fond of her in articles later. From what I experienced, they were spot on. In hindsight, I suppose she was just doing her job and doing it well. This was just another moment of having a glimpse of the INSIDE.

Yeah, that little tour was cool, but the real highlight was this group from Florida called Splack Pack, which starred this rapper named Kidd Money. Yo, their show was crazy! I had never seen naked girls on stage doing all kinds of explicit things that you only see in porn flicks. They had this song called, "Scrub the Ground." The crowd was going crazy over these dudes and it was clear that they were the tour favorites.

After it was all said and done, I had experienced my first little tour. I remember in Tampa; a guy came up to us and said that he wanted us to perform at his club in Miami the following night and would pay for our arrangements. I thought about it for a quick second and that's when reality hit me like, "I got class in the morning."

MISTER

Being that I was used to making so many dumb decisions in the past, I had to really make sure that I didn't make a move based on impulse and weigh the risks versus the reward. The risk was obvious, I was still enrolled in school, where missing class would set me back tremendously and my parents had taken out a loan for me to be there in the first place. The last thing I want to do is tell them I ditched school to try and do a show in Miami for a record deal. Not happening. The reward could be, maybe, this guy offering this opportunity was serious and knew somebody that knew somebody, that could give us a shot at a possible record deal.

It was too much of a non-guarantee, especially being that these were unpaid shows, so I still had to do what my parents sent me to school to do and Ralph had to go back home to Atlanta. We kept praying for that "record deal" that seemed to be getting real close, yet was so elusive.

Backstage Pass and Itinerary for Club Moon, opening for Outkast

Doing time in the Cipher

Check the Rhime

Back on campus, I aligned myself up with more people that were into what I was into…the music. The first guy I linked up with was a unique fellow by the name of Tee. Now Tee was what you might call the "campus clown", someone always making jokes on everybody, very social, yet irritating to most girls. He stood about 5 feet tall and wore a brown fedora hat every day. To add to that fact, he was an aspiring comedian.

Now, you're probably wondering how did I link up with this guy, right? Me too! Well to add something else to the assortment of qualities of Tee, he was a beat boxer, and a good one at that! I don't know when it started, but one day me and Tee just clicked. I would freestyle all day around campus and Tee would provide the beat box. He could also rhyme himself and would join in from time to time. I would describe his style kind of like Katt Williams' rhymes, very witty and funny.

It was one afternoon that me and Tee were leaving the cafeteria and was approached by a group of guys from the Midwest. The first guy that said something was a guy named "Ajax" or Allen Henson. He was originally from Chicago and had a reputation for killing ciphers all over campus and I had personally seen him destroy another rapper in the TV room during an episode of Rap City one day, like "DAYYAMM."

Afterwards, I spotted him outside speaking to these two cats that approached him about producing for him. I'm like, "Man, I should have rapped too!" After they were done with Ajax, I walked over to them and told them who I was and spit something for them. They were 'semi' impressed but wanted to get me in the studio with Ajax possibly. You could just tell they were more impressed with what they saw in him and who could blame them after that massacre we all witnessed in the TV room. I was thinking, I need to step my game up to get with this dude. Well, that moment of truth was about to happen here, outside the café.

He must have heard of me, because he approached on some "yo, I heard you be spitting…what u got?" Immediately, my man Tee goes into his beat box and a cipher popped off. That was the day I gained more respect for my craft and forged what would be a long-lasting friendship with all those guys that were there, which included two other guys from Milwaukee, Jrold and Day Day. Yes, Milwaukee! I was buggin, cuz I didn't even know black folks were that far north.

Anyhow, these dudes could flat out rhyme and every day you would catch us in ciphers…destroying them! Me and Ajax clicked first though, and we eventually ended up at those dude's studio that approached us, I mean him, that one day on the set. The guys' names were Mike Cork and Bill Mitchell, and their production company was called, "Low Frequencee Entertainment".

Both Mike and Bill were from Indianapolis and had high aspirations of getting into the game as producers. They just needed some artists to get it going. I'll never forget that moment at the studio. We did a freestyle session that lasted in what seemed like 'forever' and I gained a lot of respect from not only Mike, Bill, and Ajax, but from myself. I proved to myself that I could hang with this dude on the rhyme tip.

I credit Ajax with further enhancing my talent to freestyle that started with Mike and Pooh back at the crib. The main thing he did was instilling confidence in me to spit no matter who or what…just GO HARD! I recall a battle that we had on the Set with a couple of cats from a crew called Headz In The Attic. They were deep as hell and staffed with stone cold spitters.

The main guys in the crew were Khnum, M-1, and Tahir. Khnum was the most aggressive with his style. He was a real skinny dude, with a chipped tooth that looked straight grimy yo! M-1, was real deep with his flow, almost political like, but quieter. Tahir was real laid back and cool. They whole crew used to be fatigued out though! I remember Khnum did a guy in one night on campus. He had a freestyle line that ended with:

"It's like murda, u can't go no furtha
Eatin up MCs like a f**n hamburgaaaaaa"**

Yo the place went crazy off of that, coupled with the onslaught of bars that preceded that. Dude he was battling that night was stuck on stupid, straight speechless afterwards. I say all that to say, these dudes was the truth! We battled outside this spot called the Rattlers Den one night. Me and Ajax was going for ours, it was like him and Khnum going back-to-back, followed by me, M-1, and Tahir trading verses in a cipher type setting.

We left that with a whole lotta respect, which was major! They had this song they were promoting at the time called "Food, Clothes, and Shelter."

They would have the crowd participate during the hook by yelling out the main three words from the title. The song was stupid and one night at the Rattlers Den, Tahir had called me up to spit a couple of verses with them on the song. You could tell these guys were hungry and it was probably only a matter of time before somebody picked them up.

I remember we was on the Set with them one day and they were talking about dipping out of school and heading to New York to get put on. I was wishing I could bounce too, knowing good and well, THAT wasn't gonna happen. Not if Gloria Robinson and those loans she took out for me had anything to say about it. I wished them all the best of luck. If I knew then, what I would find out later, I would have told Mom "hey, I'll pay you back those loans later, I'm outta here!"

Another hot crew that was on campus was Organized Rhyme. They had two dope dudes that could straight spit from D.C. Haziq Ali was a tall, sleek guy that was just real cool. He was like a Cooley High cat with a nasal type of flow. He rarely freestyled, but his written rhymes were laced with metaphors and punchlines that were undeniable. I first met Haziq one day at the Rattlers Den while he was with another guy named DC from Jacksonville.

Now DC was arrogant as hell. Straight battle rapper, fresh dressed from head to toe. He straight brought it to like three of my guys in the Den that day. Haziq had just spit earlier, dazzling the whole crowd with his many punchlines and metaphors that he was packed with. I rhymed after him, with the off the head flow. Ajax went after me and killed it! Then, all of a sudden,

MISTER

DC breaks into the crowd points at Ajax, and two other guys with challenging verses, like What! The other two backed off, but Ajax stepped up and went head-to-head with DC. Ajax went hard with his lyrical freestyles and crazy vocabulary words that was well put together. DC just had that straight forward approach that consisted of straight disses. He broke my man down from head to toe. The killer line was when he said:

"Look at you, looking like a straight hobo
While I wear polo"

The crowd went crazy! Mainly cuz Ajax was wearing basketball shorts, rocking the sweatshirt inside out, which was no big deal, because we had just come from hooping. On any other day, Ajax was fly. However, on this day, he was dressed down…DC, on the other hand, was Polo down, from the jacket to the boots, and took advantage! Plus, he had this mean grill on his face…dude kept the Onyx face on at all times, but it was funny cuz he was a pretty boy. He showed out that day and had me looking out for him every time a cipher broke out. I wanted to make sure I was on my A game, from the clothes to the flow if he was around and really, didn't want no parts of dude after I seen what he did to one of the guys I looked up to in Ajax.

Every now and then, you would see him with Haziq in tow. It wasn't long though before we all ended up at the same studio with Low Frequencee and the freestyle session popped off. For some reason, my confidence was at an all-time high that day. Soon as I seen him in there, I just went in on a beat that was playing. I was giving it all I got too! DC got hyped as hell, like "oh, you freestyling? That's what I'm talking bout my n*gga, let's get it!"

We ended up going round for round, but not battling, just straight going for ours. Day Day was there too, so I had backup. DC gave it up to me, not knowing that he used to have me straight shook to even rhyme around him. I had brought it up about the day he battled my man Ajax and we just laughed about it. He stated that he wouldn't want to battle me though, cuz I was coming with it. I took it as a great compliment.

Haziq and I had the same round for round session at Low Frequencee's studio one day as well. That guy is just phenomenal with the lyrics, that's all I can say. His partner was a guy named Tabi Bonney, he was a native of D.C. too, but originally from Africa. Now Tabi, was just as cool as Haziq. I'm thinking what's with these cool dudes from D.C. Back home, we clashed with guys from D.C. I clicked with these guys though.

Tabi had a very smooth, soft flow and his lines were very witty. They had recorded this song for the school anthem, called "Strike Again", it was the school's alma mater. That song had a lot of buzz around campus. Organized Rhyme was doing their thing, and it wasn't long before they were singing the same tune the Headz In the Attic group was singing. They both went back to D.C. and abroad securing production and independent record deals. Haziq ended up hooking up with Roc-A-Blok records, which was home to Jay Z's producer Ski. He even put out a project with Beanie Sigel on it, back when he first hit the scene. Tabi became a successful artist as well, with songs that hit the charts.

MISTER

Meanwhile, back at the campus, Ajax and I was still recording freestyles after freestyles in the dorm rooms and at the studio with Low Frequencee. One day, I saw a flyer that announced a rapper, by the name of Supernatural, was coming to campus. I had just read about this dude in the Source Magazine. He had beat Mad Skillz in the World Rap Supremacy battle held in New York. I didn't believe how that was possible in the first place, cuz Mad Skillz was a beast on the freestyle tip! He had already been crushing mixtapes, concerts, and radio shows with his freestyle rhymes since I had last seen him in Norfolk that night!

I'm all anxious to see what this Supernatural guy is all about and see if he's really the truth. He had just battled a notorious freestyle battler in Craig G out of the Juice Crew. Though he lost, most say he really won and Craig G was really just the home crowd favorite. Me and the Midwest homies aka the Cipher Killaz were the first ones there to see this dude. They had setup a stage with four mics for this guy. Yea, I was just as puzzled, until IT happened.

This guy, no exaggerations, freestyled for four hours straight with about two curse words the whole time and one fumble on the verses! I was crazy impressed! He had the crowd throwing him objects onto the stage, while he threw it all in a rhyme and made it make sense. He even called for a few volunteers to freestyle on the stage. Now why did he do that?! WHAT?!...our whole crew hopped up there and commenced to killing it!

The most impressive moment was when Supernatural transformed his style of flow and voice to match my man Ajax's. He kicked a whole rhyme exactly how HE would have spit it! I was too impressed! If that wasn't enough, the four mics were setup for his movie that he spit starring Kurupt, Rakim, Lady of Rage, and KRS. Yes, he spit the verses and sounded exactly like them, using all four mics. I was done!!

To this date, the best I've ever witnessed in life!! I later got an autograph from him that I put in my rhyme book and still have to this day. We later spoke about how he battled Mad Skillz. He gave it up for him though, saying he was stupid with it and that it was a toss-up on the winner of the battle. Of course, I knew that, but this guy that we just witnessed, was some kind of rhyming animal with *Lyrics To Go*! Man, we couldn't stop talking about that dude for days and weeks. Of course, he fueled more ciphers and "stepping up" of our game.

Man, trust me, by the time I had left FAMU, I truly believe that there wasn't a soul alive that could compete with me, second only to both, Supernatural and Mad Skillz. The battles and cipher stories at FAMU are endless and I could go on for days with all the moments. Again, what I didn't realize, was that I was honing my performance skills, that would help with me being able to improvise during a show, by freestyling on a whim, adapting to what the crowd is giving me.

Not only that, being in the cipher builds extreme confidence for an emcee. All ears and eyes are on you, hanging on every word that you say, so it better be something that they will remember. This was a like a rap boot camp of its own. Something of which, most artists will never know anything about. In the end, it's what separates the great from the exceptional talents of the industry.

MISTER

FAMU student ID

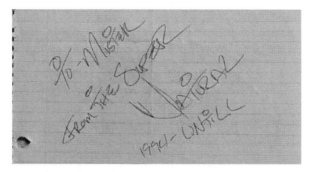

Autograph from rapper, SuperNatural

Me and Ajax

What?!

The college thing was alright. I met so many people from all over the country, forging great relationships with future leaders, that could have ended up being big time CEOs and big executives in their respective career fields. Every day was an interesting one, with something always going on.

Whether catching a game at the gym, linking up with a chick out at the library, lounging in the TV room, or just hanging out on the set. I quickly became popular on campus, from not only my name, but as the little guy from Virginia, walking around twisting his hair, with the boom box, bumping nothing but hip-hop classics.

One day, I made it back to my dorm room and my roommate was there in a panic. I asked him what was up and he said that there was two US Marshalls that showed up at the room looking for me. I was stunned, like "*What?!*" For a second, I was wondering why would anybody be here looking for me? Then it dawned on me. I had gone AWOL and they were here to pick me up and take me to jail.

I was shook and told my roommate to leave the room, so I could lock myself in it. This can't be happening! Everything was going great here at school and I was just trying to live my life. I wasn't getting into trouble anymore, or hanging with the wrong crowd, or nothing. I started praying to God and everything. At that moment, I grabbed the phone to call my Dad, who was still a high-ranking officer in the Army. Once he got on the phone,

MISTER

I told him what was going down and that I needed him to help me get out of this.

We ended up getting the commander who sent the marshals to my campus, on the phone three-way. They had me get off the phone while they talked. It wasn't long after that my Dad called me back and let me know that everything was fine. The letter that I wrote provided a great and detailed explanation for everything, and they saw fit to have me discharged.

After three and a half years, my military career was over. It was termed as a General Discharge, under Honorable Conditions, so it left me with a clean record for the military. Whew! Man, my parents are the absolute greatest. Even with all the negative drama I caused them they still had my back. I truly was blessed to have them in my corner and felt even more obligated to stay on the positive path that I was on.

Bumped plenty Hip Hop classics daily (picture with Erick Harrell (Twin)

CERTIFICATE OF RELEASE OR DISCHARGE FROM ACTIVE DUTY

1. NAME (Last, First, Middle) OVERSTREET MISTER LAVON		2. DEPARTMENT, COMPONENT AND BRANCH ARMY/ARNG		3. SOCIAL SECURITY SGL C
4.a GRADE, RATE OR RANK PFC	4.b. PAY GRADE E3	5. DATE OF BIRTH (YYMMDD) 750116	6. RESERVE OBLIG. TERM. DATE Year 2000 Month 02 Day 03	
7.a PLACE OF ENTRY INTO ACTIVE DUTY RICHMOND VA		7.b. HOME OF RECORD AT TIME OF ENTRY (City and state, or complete address if known) 207 YORKTOWN DRIVE FT LEE VA 23801		
8.a. LAST DUTY ASSIGNMENT AND MAJOR COMMAND CO L QM BDE FORT LEE VA TC		8.b. STATION WHERE SEPARATED FORT LEE, VA 23801		
9. COMMAND TO WHICH TRANSFERRED DET 1 CO C 1/183RD INF CHASE CITY VA 23924			10.-SGLI COVERAGE None Amount: $ 50,000.00	

Letter of Discharge from the military

We Can Get Down

After that huge scare, I turned my focus back to my studies and my music. Oh yeah, the mission is still in place, we gotta make it Inside baby! Ajax eventually left after Freshman year, his sister was coming up in the music industry working with the likes of Puff Daddy, Biggie, and Heavy D, so he figured he had a way in now. Besides that, he and his crew were at school but still getting down like they were back home in Chicago or something.

Most of the guys I was with were from that Midwest culture of Disciples and Vice Lords, so needless to say, there was a lot of gangster activity down at FAMU. I just couldn't seem to escape it. Here I am, all the way down in Florida, in college, of all places and it's "gangsta sh*t" popping off. I was good though…I was just a cool cat from VA who was tired of that drama I left back at home, I kept it cool with everybody. Trust me, I was over it and they can have it.

Anyhow, after Ajax left, me, Day Day, and Jrold ended up clicking up and forming a group called Cissalc. It stood for CLASSIC spelled backwards…credit Day Day for that. We were unstoppable as a group and a force to be reckoned with. I was the dynamite in the small package that was just ready to spit at any time. I thrived off a crowd being around, so I could surprise with witty and animated lines.

After all that I went thru back home in VA, my behavior at FAMU was very toned down. I smoked a lot, kept to myself and was quiet for the most part, and at other times, a straight character, clowning and just having fun. Get me to talking about anything hip-hop related, and I wouldn't shut up for hours.

Then there were these two guys from Milwaukee, Wisconsin. Jrold was the cool, laid back cat that had the "voice". It came off like a very smooth, nasal tone. So, when he rhymed, it was almost as if everything he said was slick, resembling the effortless flow that Snoop Dogg has. Jrold was also into the ladies, very much so. I mean, at FAM, we all were in a sense, but he was the more deliberate one out of us three. He had height, a fly cat that kept a fresh cut, loved playing basketball, and rocked a fresh pair of dookies damn near daily, which were a pair of Nikes. We called them Flaves in Virginia.

Day Day was around my height, but with a stockier build. Him and Jrold knew each other since like 3rd grade, they grew up together, and followed each other all the way down to Tallahassee. Day Day also was fly and kept a fresh pair of dookies on. He was, somewhat, laid back, but once he was passionate about something, he would turn all the way up. This applied to his approach in debates, playing basketball, and of course, on the mic. Very, very, aggressive.

Though I was always down for a good cipher battle, Day Day was the real problem. I remember him and Ajax had a monumental battle in the dorm room once, with neither one of them wanting to quit. I can't say who won. Let's just leave that one alone. I'll also add that, with both Day Day and Jrold, you won't win an argument or debate with either of them, so forget about it.

MISTER

I eventually introduced them both to Mike and Bill of Low Frequencee Entertainment, so the group picked up where me and Ajax left off. We started recording full demos, did radio jingles, shows, the whole nine. During this time, we went thru a whole artist development under Low Free. They booked us sessions at major studios in the city. They set us up with photoshoots for our group, to work on what they called press kits. We spent numerous occasions just sitting around, talking about the business, while learning the concepts of creating songs, from counting bars, and coming up with hooks.

I can't count all of the disagreements we would have with Mike and Bill over creativity with the songs we would do. While they were obvious students of the business side of the game, we were students of the creative side of the game, so we bumped heads quite often. Remember, you're not winning an argument or debate with Jrold and Day Day. Add me to this mix with my stubborn and anti-authority stance, and we would just have more stalemates, than any victories.

I must say, I learned a great deal under Low Frequencee and wouldn't change all of the stuff we did together for the world. As far as Cissalc goes, on the artist side of things, we were active. Any and everywhere there was a chance to grab a microphone, we took it by storm. There was no competition in our eyes, and arguably, there wasn't another group doing it bigger than us at that time.

We even did campus sets with an up-and-coming DJ that went by the name of DJ Demp. He had this event called "Demp Week" that he started up where it would be seven days' worth of partying and events. We were right there at every function performing and impressing the crowds. Now it wouldn't be fair if I failed to mention our moment of failure as opposed to glory.

There was this gong show styled event that was held in the Lee Auditorium. This was the same location, where filmmakers, Rob Hardy and Will Packer, debuted their first movie, called "Chocolate City." They were members of the Alpha Phi Alpha fraternity and major players on campus. Will also served as president of the SGA, which was the same student body that would be instrumental in getting me kicked out of FAMU. It seems school wasn't for me.

Anyhow, the audience was about 800 to 1000 people in Lee Auditorium. We had to do a set with DJ Kool Ant, who invited us to perform with him. We were totally convinced that we were going to kill the show. Now, everybody that went up that night got booed for some odd reason. I figured they was getting booed because they were whack and deserved it anyway. Well, now the moment of truth was here!

Kool Ant was already setup on stage before we got up there to do an intro. Right when he started his intro, the crowd automatically was getting ready to boo. We took the stage and as soon as Day Day went into his verse, the crowd starting booing. I was stunned, mainly because we already made a name for ourselves on campus and felt we had a crowd of supporters. Even with a gang of our crew there, the boos bled across the auditorium. I screamed into the mic to stop the music and to quiet everybody down:

MISTER

"yall wait a minute, I don't know what yall thinking
But this is Cissalc, real hip hop s**t, yall ain't booing this
tonight"

The crowd had gotten completely silent while I was talking, and it seemed like they all took a deep breath at the same time. It was as if you could actually hear the inhale that ended with a loud and boisterous "BOOOOOOOOOOOOOO!!" I threw the mic down and we rushed off the stage. My first "booed off the stage" moment.

Backstage, we were devastated. I'm talking about cursing and damn near crying at the same time. I'll never forget that moment, because it built us and made us stronger. After a while, we shook it off and understood that it was a Gong Show and people just wanted to have fun and boo everybody anyway. No one made it through a complete set that night. Even though we had gotten booed off stage, that was a very minor setback.

We kept the momentum going, kept doing more shows, and kept it moving with campus buzz. Low Frequencee set us up with a featured interview for the local paper with an up-and-coming journalist named, Keith Murphy, out of Chicago. It was a major accomplishment because everybody got that article and it had major circulation throughout the city. I kept copies of it and sent it to family and friends, I was so proud of my first interview.

Keith went on to become a major writer for Blaze and Vibe magazine. He's interviewed all the top dogs of the industry, so I'm happy to be part of his resume as one of his first interviews when he was on the come up at FAMU.

Cissalc was on the rise and it felt great. Not only our group, but our whole crew were like THE big men around campus, even as Freshmen. We were invited to mostly all of the Senior class events, because they were run by all the big homies who were all from the Midwest regions. A lot of the fraternity brothers and sorority sisters would invite us to perform at their parties as well.

We had crew, looks, and the swag to go with it. We had the songs to match too. The most popular of all our records, was a song called "To Be Continued" and another one titled "You Don't Know Me". These two songs were the cream of the crop and circulated around campus. We even did solo songs.

The very first solo song that I ever recorded was with Low Frequencee. It was called a "Dime And a Nickel." I blasted that song in my boom box for weeks around campus and had it buzzing. Not to be outdone, Day Day followed with a solo song of his own, then Jrold came with his.

All of the solo songs were smashes and before you know it, most everybody was bumping those records, along with some other new recordings like "Corral The Scent" and "The Luau", which ended up being the first song I ever heard played in the Club and on the radio. I remember being on Florida State's campus at one of their parties. We were getting ready to leave in our cars, and all of a sudden, "The Luau" came on the radio. We jumped out the cars wilding out, like "that's us, that's our song!"

It brought me back to that feeling I had as a kid. I used to wonder how these unique beings found a way to get inside my radio. I always wanted to know how to do that. To hear my voice coming thru this alien atmosphere of radio waves, gave me a sense of uniqueness and separation from the rest of the world.

At that time, and even now in most cases, there weren't many people who could say that they're on the radio, or even know someone that was on the radio. We're not even going to get into television or movies right now. Just to crack the seal of being on the radio is viewed to most, as a once in a lifetime thing or dream. "The Luau" was the song that gave me that first experience.

We had collaborated on that song with a crew called Southside Pride that my man Jamaal Rose was a part of. Jamaal was actually from Tallahassee and was one of the first people in the city, that provided us with opportunities to get known locally. He was very close to us and made it a point to keep us heavily involved in the local music scene.

The Luau was an actual event that was sponsored by the Kappa Alpha Psi fraternity. It was the largest event of the year. We both recorded and performed the theme song for it, to a crowd that numbered in the hundreds at an outside venue. I'm telling you, Cissalc, was IT.

The shows we were doing gained us a lot of campus popularity as being one of the premier groups on the scene. We even did a show with Goodie Mob, Xscape, and Lil Jamal when they came to campus. I remember running up on Lil Jamal, like "wassup man."

He jumped and looked at me all crazy, like he was ready to throw down. I was totally thrown off by that. He then said he thought I was Havoc from Mobb Deep. At the time, Mobb Deep had this beef going on with Keith

Murray and Def Squad. I then remembered reading about him having a run-in with the Mobb out in Queensbridge a while back. That moment was weird and funny at the same time.

Shout out to my man, Moet aka Majada the Prez, FAMU alum who was also a cipher killa. He was holding Lil Jamal down on stage later that day, dude was sick with the flow too. Majada and I had a few moments of rocking together ourselves. We hit the city up one night, bored as hell probably, and ended up in this all-white club. We walked in and saw nothing but white folks all over, I mean, straight sticking out like Kit Kats in a glass of milk.

We didn't care at all! We made our way to the back of the bar area and noticed a live band performing. Now, the live band had like two black guys in it and the rest of the bandmembers were white. They had mics setup in front of them, but no vocalists?? We all looked at each other and didn't think twice about it.

Next thing you know, we're on the mic rocking with the live band, in a club full of white folks, KILLING it!! They were up on their feet, clapping their hands, some on beat…some not. It didn't matter, we all had a good time that night. The name of the band was called FUNKEVANGELISTS. They gave it up for us freestyling the whole night and the crowd gave us nothing but standing ovations. That was another moment of me having this feeling of surreal after noticing that I could appeal to a whole different crowd of people.

It was another time I rocked the Lee Auditorium. Yep, the same spot where we had just gotten booed. On this particular night, I was straight feeling the moment. I had Jrold lend me his red Kangol hat, that hung over my eyes like LL. I had the black and white fatigue vest on to go with it. It just so happened that my microphone had the red foam top to it that matched perfectly!

The curtains opened and it was ShowTime. We used the Smif n Wessun track from "Let's Get It On" and rocked out. I did my part and noticed the whole crew down on the floor by the front of the stage. I went into the crowd and walked up between the isles, gettin it yo!

On my way back, I passed the mic to an eagerly waiting Day Day, who popped off the cipher session starring himself, Jrold, and host of others. We owned Lee Auditorium that night!! Man, nobody could see Cissalc in any shape or form. Who can forget the time when Boot Camp Clik came to campus…it was stupid.

We were one of the few that got to chill and chop it up with the likes of Buckshot, Smif n Wesson, and Redman. It was a trip, because Dru Ha was like "hey, yall got that new Da Shinin Album?" He just didn't know who he was talking to. We had the album right there in our walk-mans! We pulled it out like, "what!"

Later that night at the show, Redman put a challenge out for anybody to battle his man Lil Jamal for a stack. I was more than willing to do it, only problem is, I didn't have a STACK. Hey, students are broke. He talking bout a stack, I didn't even have ten dollars in my pocket. I had already spent my net check from my loans on food and weed! Crazy times, man!

I so envied those guys and fiend greatly to be in their shoes one day. "My time is coming soon, I know it" I would always say to myself. Cissalc would go onto be in rotation on Tallahassee's local radio station, 90.5, thanks to a radio promo we did for the station called "90.5 Gettin Live." Having your voice heard on the radio, never gets old. We had already had our song, "The Luau" debut on the local radio station, to now we're being played weekly!

It was dope to have everyone on the campus coming up to us, saying they heard the song. We were some real celebs on campus, enjoying all the activities of such, as one could imagine...being a teenager, all black college campus, no curfew or parents, yeah, you get the point.

We also did phenomenal mixtapes with a then DJ Nyce aka Khari Cain. He's now known as producer Needlz who has worked with everyone from 50 Cent to Bruno Mars. I had also joined the Almighty Zulu Nation at that time and was enlightening myself with all types of different culture and people from different backgrounds. All of that would play a part in my whole development as a writer and rap artist, and really gave me an appreciation and true understanding for the culture of Hip Hop.

MISTER

A clip from article in the FAMUAN of Cissalc

Performing at the Kappa Luau (RIP Jamaal Rose)

Mind Power

A lot of the lessons I learned at FAMU, contributed a great deal to the content of everything that I wrote. I went thru a huge period of enlightenment, where I would study and research a wide range of philosophical and economical ideologies, in an effort to gain an understanding of the world I was living in and my own individual purpose.

Though my main interest was always about getting into the music industry, there has been a constant unsettling of my soul that I would have. I know that there's much more to life and that we all have a purpose. For the most part, I was trying to find myself and wanted to know exactly "why I'm here."

I would even write a mini-book titled as such, giving my reasons as to why I believe I was put here on Earth. If I'm losing any of you right now, I totally get it. I come from a different time to where we would often just sit around and do what we call "building." There was nothing like a good session of smoking out, vibing to some Poor Righteous Teachers, Wutang Clan, Brand Nubian, or Rass Kass, while dissecting their verses and discovering all types of different information that was passed thru those speakers. After which, we would usually break out into a freestyle session.

Around my second year at school, I had moved out of the campus dorms and started living off campus with Day Day and Jrold in an apartment complex called Mabry Village. The three of us roomed together, however, I didn't have a room, so I slept on the couch, next to the stereo of course. These were the best of times, as we went thru every struggle possible, as well as, partied.

It was during this time, that I would document everything by recording our "building" and freestyle sessions and turned them into what I would call my very own mixtapes. These tapes would literally just be recordings of us just hanging out at Mabry, playing video games, watching sports, debating, clowning, and of course freestyling.

Mostly everybody hated my mixtapes and thought I was doing too much by recording everything, which could be seen as a nuisance, I suppose. I always said that my mixtapes would blow up one day once we got big, to which a straight clown session would follow. I just wanted to have these moments captured, just to listen to later, on my own time. It's something I often did at home with my sister and brother, so it was normal to me.

I didn't think nothing of it. Ask me the value of these 'mixtapes' today. Let's just say, I got the last laugh. No worries, they'll be available on a streaming platform near you…soon! Man, I miss those days.

As far as the situation with Low Frequencee turned out, we felt that although we were doing a little bit here and there with the music, they just didn't have enough to take us to the next level of where we really wanted to go, or at least we didn't see it that way. That way of thinking was so off the mark and I charge it to being ignorant to how the game actually worked.

We're just thinking that some major label like Def Jam or LaFace would notice us and we would sign this major deal. At that time, we thinking like, 'sign a deal, then it's hoes, shows, and dough'. So, when the paperwork was presented to us to sign a production deal with Low Frequencee Entertainment, we died laughing, like are you kidding me? "Yall ain't no major label…we ain't signing our life away to y'all, for what?!"

It didn't help that all the legal jargon of the contracts is enough to scare anyone, like just forget about it. If it ain't a major, it ain't worth the risk…we ain't doing it. We were really just amped off of our visits to Atlanta with Ralph and about the movement we were forming. It was just so much more opportunity there and we, at least I, figured to give that a shot before I signed anything.

All I could think about when they presented the contracts, was the famous line from Q-Tip of A Tribe Called Quest, where he said "Industry rule number 4080, record company people are shadyyy." Plus, we were looking at these guys, like y'all trying to get in just like us. The thought of coming up as a team from the bottom never struck us…ala, Organized Noize, Wutang Clan, Death Row, etc.

At the end of the day, even without a production deal, these guys did all the things for us, as artists, that you're supposed to get *after* signing a production deal. They really believed, invested, and made a commitment to us prior to even presenting an offer for us to do the same. After all that they did, we should have felt obligated to sign the contract on the strength of the investment they had already made alone.

You have to think about the money that was spent for studio time, producing tracks, paying for photoshoots, setting up interviews for publications, teaching us the business side of the game. Again, they were still learning the game just like us. Had they really been on their business, we wouldn't have said one word on that mic, prior to signing an agreement. Perhaps they did know, however, and just wanted to give these hungry kids a chance to do what they love.

Either way, we both learned a lot from each other, and it was a great relationship that we still have to this day. Shout out to "Macork" and "Pushy", Mike is currently doing exceptionally well as a highly sought-after photographer in Tallahassee.

The last time I saw Bill, he was working as a mixing engineer at some of the major studios in Atlanta. He has put in work with Jazze Pha and worked with MCA records for their artists as well. Bill ended up being very instrumental in a pivotal moment during my journey. Just want to acknowledge those guys and thank them for everything. I appreciate yall's efforts, fa real!

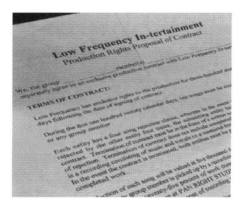

Production-Artist contract presented by Low Frequency Entertainment

Posted up in Mabry Village (Malcus, Durand, Cissalc)

With future Grammy winning producer Needlz (then, DJ Nyce)

Keeping It Moving

After about two years in college, barely attending classes, and being broke struggling as a student/rap artist, I was getting real antsy about leaving and moving to Atlanta, where things were really getting big on the music tip. Ralph was still there and trying to get me to move there and bang out with him.

Initially, the agreement was for us, Cissalc, to all leave school and head to Atlanta to get this record deal. Though, that was the plan, I ended up being the only one to make the move. I eventually pulled my version of Kanye and dropped out of college to pursue the music fulltime.

My parents, grandparents, well, the majority of my whole family was upset about it. What I also didn't mention, was that I was kicked out of school for being part of a massive protest that opposed the president of the University and his entire administration for misappropriating financial aid funds for students. Years later, that same administration, would end up getting fired after it was discovered that they were doing just that.

The protest I was involved in, ended up being a huge deal, that led to many arrests, charges pressed, and students kicked out. I was one of them. I was fined and my transcripts were put on hold, preventing me from re-enrolling at the school. This also meant I would have to start from scratch at another school. I was over the whole school thing anyway.

At the end of the day, I just wanted to rap! I figured that the only thing that would bring me any satisfaction out of life, would be to pursue and accomplish my goal, not dream, of getting in this industry.

Once I left school, I had every intention of moving to Atlanta, but I still hadn't quite figured out a way to make it happen. I refused to regroup in Florida with family, so I made a detour, back to VA, where I would waste more time of doing pretty much of nothing but stayed out of trouble for the most part. I kept a very low profile. Still, I was focused on my goal of making something happen with the music.

Back when I was still enrolled at FAMU, there was a hip-hop group from the West Coast by the name of The B.U.M.S that had a tour stop in Tallahassee. The B.U.M.S had a record out called "Free My Mind" that was getting a lot of airplay on Rap City. Sway and King Tech, who were very large in the bay area in California, were very instrumental in getting them their start.

I had an opportunity to connect with them during a meet and greet on campus. They were very cool and down to earth. One of the rappers, Evol, had given me his contact info and said he would stay in touch. I have to admit that I didn't really think they would actually do so, until they showed up in my hometown of Petersburg, out of all places, for a show.

Once I caught wind that they were in town, I called the number I had for Evol and he answered. He told me to meet him outside the club and I could get in with them. Now, this was a big deal for sure to walk past everyone in the line. Once the carpool pulled up with the featured artists of the night, The B.U.M.S stepped out the ride and I called out for Evol. He saw me and waved for me to walk in with them. You couldn't tell me NOTHING!

They rocked the crowd and I had front row seats to witness it. We later chilled out with a few groupies back at the hotel in Richmond. I listened to their tour stories and was totally fascinated by the lifestyle. I appreciate those guys for following up and giving me an opportunity to kick it with them, if only for that one moment.

One of the DJs at the venue they had performed at was Lonnie B, from Richmond. I remember Lonnie B from being one of the guys that ran with Mad Skillz and was also a part of the infamous MC battle that Supernatural eventually won. I introduced myself to him and we exchanged info as well.

This would lead to me linking with him later at his house somewhere off Chippenham Pkwy, where we would kick verses and talk about the music game. Of course, I had mentioned to him about how Mad Skillz had put me on at his open mic showcase back in the day and that I was digging their movement. Lonnie B was a superb lyricist and had this effortless delivery with crazy punchlines.

He and Mad Skillz were part of a collective called the Supafriendz, which consisted of talented emcees in the Richmond area, known for witty rhymes and freestyling. Linking up with Lonnie B, in my mind, was definitely a step in the right direction.

Things were gradually beginning to come into place. Meanwhile, I was everywhere from Petersburg, to Richmond, to Hampton, to VA Beach getting into all types of drama, while at the same time, jumping in any cipher, and rapping for anybody who would listen. I studied the game, I wrote more and more rhymes, and kicked it a lot.

It was pretty obvious that the distractions of the streets, and non-opportunities in Virginia, would certainly not benefit me and my plans of making it on the Inside. It was becoming very frustrating, yet I stayed hungry! I ended up getting a job at MCI in Newport News off of Warwick Blvd, working part time. Ralph kept begging me to get out of VA and get to Atlanta. The opportunity came in the form of a job transfer. They told me that they had a branch in Atlanta, so I put in a request to be relocated.

I'll never forget it, around that time, Tupac had just been shot up and I had just received confirmation of my transfer on the Friday that he died. I remember my last night at work up there, riding home and listening to Big B and Kool DJ Law on 102.9 talking about the death of this rap legend that shocked the industry and the entire world. It was a sad moment.

I kicked it with my homie Al and his Air Force buddies on Langley Base, getting drunk off Thug Passion drinks all day and for the rest of the week! After a week of mourning one of the greatest artists of our time, it was time for self-reflection. "Mister, we gotta get Inside…what are YOU doing for YOUR legacy?" At this point, I'm not exactly sure, but I'm optimistic. Atlanta, GA, here I come!

MISTER

Me and DJ Lonnie B

Business card I received from DJ Lonnie B

The Hop

Atlanta, Georgia. A Black metropolis and melting pot of people from all over the country that have decided to transplant, after discovering this goldmine of a city. The music scene was exploding with labels, such as So So Def (Jermaine Dupri, Kris Kross, Xscape, Da Brat), LaFace (Toni Braxton, TLC, Usher, Outkast, Goodie Mob) and Rowdy (Dallas Austin, Monica, ABC).

Hip Hop artists from everywhere were recording their music in Atlanta (Puff Daddy, Busta Rhymes, Tupac, Too Short, Erick Sermon, Redman, BIG). Major industry events such as Jack the Rapper and even Freaknik brought major visitors from everywhere. It was normal to spot a celebrity like heavyweight boxing champ, Evander Holyfield at the gas station, or Halle Berry at the local grocery store, or bump into Keith Sweat at the mall.

The nightlife was insane. Strip clubs like Magic City, Club Nikki's, Gentleman's Club, and Strokers were normal gathering spots for networking and good food. Oh yeah, the women were great to look at too…very talented women I might add. Other popular spots such as Club 559, 112, Club Kaya, and Atlanta Live were a must to attend from downtown, thru Midtown, all the way up to Buckhead.

Pimps, dope dealers, gangsters, and entertainers can all be found in one venue at any given time. This is the era of the rising Black Mafia Family, the Red Dogs, robbing crew, and nights at the Cascade skating rink. Anybody who's Anybody found themselves in Atlanta at some point to make something happen, to party, or to just see what the hell is going on here!

The allure of this city I had already experienced prior, when me and Al came down for Freaknik. It was always a goal to get back here as soon as possible. I took a slight detour with going to college, but now the moment is here, wassup ATL!

My job transfer didn't consist of any moving costs and I didn't have much to move anyway. I made my way down to Florida to visit family first. My mother definitely wasn't feeling the decision but being that I had been kicked out of FAMU for protesting, I was really unable to return. With no money and a need to get to Atlanta, I made *The Hop* on a Greyhound bus at about midnight out of Gainesville, Florida, then arrived right at the bus station across from Magic City.

Ralph met me there and we caught the MARTA back to College Park. I moved in with Ralph and his mother in Kings Gate apartments, where we toughed it out until, after about a month, we moved into our own spot off Camp Creek Pkwy. We had the studio setup in the crib, so it was nonstop recording. We formed a movement with a few other people that we were hanging around at the time called BOGOD, which stood for Brothers Out Getting Over Daily.

The crew consisted of: Big Cheese, a wild and charismatic dude from Bronx, NY. Everybody knew Cheeseburger. Skittles, also from Bronx, NY...she was a monster freestyler and could really write! Tenille "Bird" from Tennessee, who could also write and rap. Cam aka "Red Eye da Addicted" ...can't remember where he was from. Then there was Chris

"Low Down" Foster from St. Nicholas Projects, Harlem, NY. He was a monster producer and would regularly collab or compete with Ralph on the beat tip! To add to this, was of course, myself and Cissalc, Ralph, Krook and Pooh straight from home, VA! With the exception of maybe half of us, about 9 of us all lived in that 2-bedroom apartment in the Diplomat off of Camp Creek Pkwy.

My homie Krook, was fresh off a robbery and wanted for a murder charge while he was in the A, so everything he did had a sense of extreme urgency. Needless to say, he was the driving force and Ralph was the foundation of the whole movement. We made so many songs that I still have a majority of all of them on cassette tapes and four-track tapes.

Speaking of the four-track tapes, we recorded on a Tascam 4-track machine that I had purchased from the Guitar Center up HWY 85 for Ralph. It was back while I was still at FAMU that me and DayDay drove up to Atlanta to visit Ralph.

I had just got a MasterCard that most students are bombarded with once they get to college. I had a $500 limit on the card and spent $400 of it on that 4-track. I remember asking Ralph what we needed to record while at the Guitar Center and he pointed it out. I said, "I can just use my credit card." He gave me this look like 'fa real?' I was like, why not? I remember him saying something like, "I gotchu for life for getting this yo". It was that serious at the time. Of course, I never paid that credit card off, but we had something to record on. We did about 2 songs before we went back to FAMU on that trip. I still have those songs too.

MISTER

Back to the matter at hand, we made countless songs in an attempt to get them to different record Executives. Ralph came across this book that had all the addresses for every label and we just started sending demos out, by mail. We even went door to door at the record labels in Atlanta. No luck! We tried every window possible to get in the door.

I recall a day when me, Krook, and Pooh went downtown to look for Erick Sermon's rim shop that was in his video, "Stay Real". It's amazing how much you can learn just by watching videos. We found the rim shop on the corner of Ralph McGill and Peachtree St. It had all types of crazy rims hanging up in the windows. For some crazy reason, we thought that we would just walk in and see Erick Sermon off top! Yea, right!

We went in and saw some dude working at the counter. He asked if we were interested in getting some rims…we all looked at each other, like 'this guy'. "Naw man, we came here looking for Erick Sermon…we a rap group from Virginia, does he ever come in here?" Dude was like, "yea, he does from time to time…but he's not here today". The guy then says that Lil Jamal was in the back though. We got all excited, like "whaattt…tell that n***a to come out here!"

Lil Jamal was formerly of the young group Illegal, but currently signed as a solo artist with Dallas Austin's label, Rowdy Records and a part of Def Squad! This was definitely a great consolation prize to not seeing Erick Sermon. Besides, I hadn't seen Lil Jamal since FAMU, when he had mistaken me for Havoc of Mobb Deep. There was no doubt in mind, that he wouldn't remember that moment at all.

The dude calls for him to come up front and in walks Lil Jamal aka Mally G. He comes out and greets us like, "wassup y'all". We replied excitedly, "wassup Mally", as if we had known this guy for years. Krook always had a natural knack for gelling with people quick, he just had that type of charisma about him. Somehow, we found ourselves in the car with Lil Jamal and his partner, a guy named Oklahoma, riding thru the city of Atlanta! This was, by far, one of the most memorable moments in our history in Atlanta!

Riding around the city with Lil Jamal proved to be both exciting and very informative. We found out while rolling with this dude, just how talented he really was on the writing and freestyle tip. He took us all over the city, telling us stories about him and Lil Malik of Illegal and how they broke up. He mentioned that they really didn't have any beef at all. He just said that they went out to L.A. for a while and Malik just said he was staying out there with Snoop and wasn't coming back. That was the end of the group.

He also told us how Left Eye was the reason he came to Atlanta. She took him in and took care of him, when he was on the streets. He spoke about how he used to hang with Pac when he lived in Atlanta and how he used to take his mother, Afeni Shakur's, trash out for her and carry her groceries.

He talked about the incident between him and Mobb Deep that went down in Queensbridge at a video shoot. He said that he didn't even know he was in Queensbridge when they ran up on him. This was during the publicized beef between Def Squad and Mobb Deep at the time.

MISTER

He schooled us on who he thought was the best emcees to come out of Philly. He said that "Kurupt is one of the illest n****z out of Philly", Will Smith was not hood but highly respected, and that the nicest emcee, besides himself, out of Philly was Black Thought! He told us how him and Shyheim was real tight and that they were going to make an album together as Lil Mef and Lil Red, after Method Man and Redman, of course!

He went on to talk about how he used to run with Treach and his whole squad in Jersey! He also said that "Keith Murray is one of the wildest n****z out" and they used to get into it all the time. He also spoke about how Redman was his big brother and that he'd do anything for him and Erick Sermon.

As irony would have it, while he was rambling on his tales of the industry, he yells out "hey, there go E right there…turn the car around, turn the car around!" We in the back, looking at each other, like "is this for real?" We came out looking for this man and Lil Jamal is going to take us directly to him! Oklahoma turned the car around and Lil Jamal flagged the white Lexus truck down that was in front of us.

We pulled over to the side of the street and Mally hopped out the car to run over to the Lexus truck! We all looked over and saw with our own eyes, "hey, Erick Sermon, hey!" It was the green-eyed bandit in the flesh! Krook was amped and ready to get out and holler at him, but Oklahoma stopped the whole show. He was like, "yo, you don't wanna do that right now…they got business they trying to handle…don't worry, yall rolling with the Squad, yall will see him again soon."

Now, any other time, we wouldn't care what anybody said, we going in! Oklahoma sold us on the fact that Mally doesn't just pick up anybody off the streets at random and that we were definitely down with "the Squad!" It didn't help that we were in a coupe and had to be let out the back seat of the car either. Me and Pooh waited on Krook's move…if he didn't move, we didn't move. After all, he was the most aggressive out of the three of us, so we respected his call. He agreed with Oklahoma and decided to play it smart, by just remaining cool.

By this time, Mally G came back to the car all excited from the conversation he just had with "E Dubb!" He said that he told Erick Sermon about us already and that we were about to make some big moves, "don't worry, y'all with me man…y'all with the Squad right now!" For some reason, the more they said that, the more we were sold and happy as hell at our opportunity to finally have found a door to get IN!

From there, he took us to this studio somewhere out on the East part of town in Decatur. The engineer at the studio was excited to see Mally and they chopped it up about the recent loss of Pac. The engineer went on to play some exclusive songs that were just recorded by the Outlawz. They were some pretty hot songs too! When we left the studio, Mally went to pick up an ounce of good green, that I was tempted to smoke, but didn't.

I had just set a New Year's resolution to not smoke any weed for the year, to see how long it would last. It didn't last long, but Krook helped me to not relapse that day in the car. He basically said, "you gonna break a promise to yourself over a little smoke with Lil Jamal?" The way he said it, put it all in perspective and made a lot of sense.

Anyhow, Mally kept telling us that he had a show to do out of town and he wanted us to go with him. Now this seemed to be the best news yet! We get to go on the road with Mally G?! This was all too good to be true! He basically said that we would have to ride out there with him to perform, but we would be gone for about a week or so.

Problem…we all had jobs that was helping to pay for our rent and bills on Camp Creek Pkwy and we were broke! There is no way that we can afford to hit the road with Mally, unless he was paying us to go…he wasn't! Oklahoma waited for Mally to get out the car at another stop, to explain that we could catch the next show and that he needed to get Mally back to the crib.

Basically, what he was saying was, 'he ain't ever going to tell y'all to leave, because he can kick it all day everyday…but he has some business that he needs to take care of and we don't need to be in the way of that'. It was then that we realized that Oklahoma was more than just Mally's homie and driver. He was a strong support system that helped Mally stay focused and on task. It was beginning to look like this whole day of fun was just that…a day of fun with a rapper! Reality struck within days of not hearing back from Lil Jamal on that Monday to hit the road or at all, for that matter. We had Oklahoma's number as well and he wasn't answering or returning phone calls.

Damn! We should have hopped out and went for broke with Erick Sermon when we had the chance! All in all, there is no regretting or forgetting that day we spent with Lil Jamal and I don't care what nobody says, he's one of the real ones in the industry! Anyway, it was back to the drawing board.

MISTER

Diplomat Apartments, Apt #85…Off Camp Creek Pkwy

Big Cheese

Day Day, Ralph and Chris

Big Skittles (on Right)

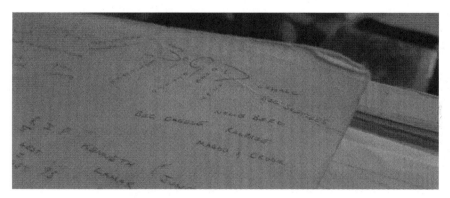

B.O.G.O.D. (Brothers Out Getting Over Daily)

Push It Along

With no success on the music side of things, the party side of things was great! In Atlanta, it's not hard at all to mingle and hang out with the stars at hardly no cost at all. I remember me, Larry, Al, and Krook all went to Nas' triple platinum party for "It Was Written". It was also Shaka Zulu's birthday party. Shaka was well known in Atlanta and contributed a great deal to the Atlanta music scene.

Pooh had just come home and told us about him meeting Nas at the airport where he worked at and he was bragging to Nas about how good his homie Krook was on the mic. Pooh had us all laughing at Nas' reply, "oh yea? He pushing brooms like you too dun?" haha…we couldn't stop laughing at that man.

Versace was a big deal then, so Al hooked me up with some gear he bought, Larry hooked up Krook in a suit and we hit the party at a spot called Atlanta Live in Buckhead! Man, we partied it up, literally, with everybody from Nas, Capone and Noreaga, Mary J Blige, Nick Van Exel, Penny Hardaway, Allen Iverson, you name it.

The funniest was when we ran into Tracey Lee and Krook tried to battle him right on the spot. Tracey Lee was like, "look man, I don't battle…I'm just blessed to be in this position…I went to school with BIG's manager." He gave us his number, but we never caught up with him after that. Industry 101, baby! It was not strange for something like that to happen, and often.

I met Rico Wade once and he gave me his phone number, to the office of course, and told me to call him on such and such day to meet. I was all excited, had a full demo tape ready. I called him, he answered and told me what day to come to the office. I'm super geeked up to finally have a chance opportunity, get there, and Rico is out of town…somewhere in Puerto Rico. The secretary told me that he said to leave the tape there at the office and he would contact me later. I'm still waiting.

Another time was when I met Mr. Cheeks at a club. He kicked it with me the whole night on some cool sh*t, gave me his personal number and the number to his manager, Charles Suitt. Well, his number ended up being changed and Mr. Suitt gave me the biggest runaround through his office personnel. I could go on and on with examples like this and that was EARLY in the game. I found the music fraternity to be the hardest thing ever to get into.

Meanwhile, Krook finally got caught and extradited back to VA and was convicted of murder, serving time in NC. Pooh went back home to VA disappointed and back to the streets. The whole BOGOD camp split up in all directions. Ralph was dealing with a whole different issue, that I will elect for him to write about in his book. Nevertheless, his situation ended up hurting us a lot because he was the foundation for everything.

With my partners in crime gone, I was left to start recording on my own. I hooked up with this white kid named Scott Weatherwax, who would open his home studio to me for massive recordings. Scott used to work with me at a job I had called Booth Research, which was one of the coolest jobs I ever had. It was a call center out in Dunwoody, ran by black people, but a front office ran by white people that paid us every Friday like clockwork. All we did was make calls and conduct surveys for $11 an hour…easy!

I spent most my time writing rhymes at my cubicle and freestyling in the break room. Scott held an IT position there. He was also an aspiring DJ, producer, and one of the most honest music critics I had ever met. He actually had a chance to meet Krook, when he had a short stint working at Booth, before he got sent up. I actually took Krook to Scott's studio to record one of his records called "Feel Me" at that time. Krook respected Scott's honesty and his bar none critique of music. He was an asshole, but in a good way.

I mean, I would write the sickest bars and put together my proudest song and let him hear it like, "hey, Scott check this song out man…I just did it the other night, it's hot!" Scott would listen and be like, "yea, it's a'ight, but I've heard better…the beat could be more like…I mean, if that's what you're going for, then cool". Haha, dude was straight raw with it.

His parents were loaded and had a nice crib out in Norcross, where Scott kept the studio. Back then, we were just moving from the reel-to-reel era over to the digital recording. Scott's studio was the first place where I recorded digitally using a program called Cakewalk. He used to make these mixtapes that he passed out around the Northside of Atlanta, on Roswell Rd and Northridge.

He had other artists he was working with as well, like Khari, Kwan the Don, the Leprechauns, and Raw Footage. Raw Footage consisted of my man, Reality and Q. I met Reality at Booth Research also, along with a guy named Tone, who rapped in a group called Mass Influence and another guy named Big Von. Big Von stood about 6'7" tall or so. He could draw real good, but also could rhyme.

We were all aspiring artists in there, but I remember Reality from a showcase that we both were apart of years ago at the Club Warehouse, in downtown Atlanta. At that time, I was just visiting Ralph and we went to the showcase searching for a chance to perform in front a host of industry executives and artists. That was the first con we fell for. A showcase, where we pay $25 to register and they have *invited* guests of every label and rap star in the game. The key word is "invited" guests! I'll never forget the guy's name who had us rehearsing and acting like it was a major event…Quazar! What a scam, but I would find out that it was all a part of the hustle in this game.

I brought that up to Reality when we met, in which he recalled that 'bs' as well! Moving along, we all would collaborate and mash out on these mixtapes. I can't lie, the white boy had it going on with the mixtapes! In addition to the mixtapes, Scott would give me beats to write to, which helped me work on penning actual songs.

These same songs I would record with at the studio with Scott who would bounce the songs to tape. After that, we would go to his car in the garage and do the "car test" to make sure the mix was right. The final stop would be Al's Infinity J30 Bose speakers. If it didn't bump in there, I would go back to the drawing board. I used to hate the anxiety I would have when getting Al and Larry to listen to my music once I recorded it. Getting my music to make it pass them two was the real fire.

MISTER

For the time being, I was making progress and had a few favorites that I recall. There was the first single, "This is Hot" that carried a cool melody hook. The next song was "Something Called A Passion", which is very laid back and all-around feel-good record talking about my love for hip hop music. Another standout is "Live At The White Owl", a record that Larry even jumped on and did adlibs.

It was a fun time of songwriting and getting the chance to hone my skills, all while having my own music to ride to. Thru Scott, I was able to put together an EP of songs that I would use as a demo to get heard, so shout out to Scott Weatherwax...who's doing it big now with his multimedia company, Mindzai!

I recall being at work one day, when Reality gave me a sampler from Loud records. It had songs from various Loud artists from Wutang Clan, Mobb Deep, Big Pun, and a new group called Dead Prez. The song Dead Prez had on the sampler was called "Food, Clothes, and Shelter." I'm thinking, "naw, It can't be." That was the song that Headz in The Attic had back at FAMU.

I didn't know if it was them or not, even after I heard the song because they sounded a little different...different as in "polished". Everything was confirmed once I saw a pic of M-1 and Khnumn in the Source Magazine modeling some Helly Hanson gear, with Lord Jamar of Brand Nubians in the background.

Apparently, they had run into Lord Jamar, who linked them with Steve Rifkind for a deal on Loud. They had changed their names to Stic Man and M1, collectively known as Dead Prez. "They did it!" I was happy for them, yet so disappointed that I hadn't made it happen yet. They had the guts to drop out of school, dip from Florida and go all the way up top to New York City and make it happen, just like they said they would, WOW!

Here I am at Booth Research, doing customer service work, calling people trying to get them to do some surveys at $11/hr. and these guys were out rocking, doing shows, and living it! Come to find out, Lord Jamar was Reality's first cousin, and he had already known about Dead Prez and their deal. To hear him and others talk about how dope these guys were and for me to actually have history with them, was so heartbreaking, bittersweet in a sense, yet an affirmation that I belonged and just as capable of being on the other side of that glass.

I immersed myself into the music even more. I was everywhere rapping and performing. Pooh had just moved back to Atlanta for another stint, so we teamed up to knock out some more music. I did my best to try and fill the void that Krook had left and with that as motivation, I was relentless in my approach of attacking this music game. Me and Pooh connected and formed a cool chemistry, with him being the boisterous and aggressive one, while I was in my wordplay and narrative bag. We were a perfect ying and yang mixture that produced a lot of great songs that would turn into a project called "Shandaleer."

My man Neal Kelly, who we met thru Ralph, had hooked up an enhanced cd that we used as our demo and press kit. It was definitely ahead of its time. An enhanced cd was capable of playing both your music and visuals. You could put it into a cd player and in your computer, in which you could have a bio, pictures, and video setup for viewing.

This was a very unique way to package a music demo and I felt good being one of the few, if not the only, artist, signed or unsigned that had it. Given the little bit of momentum we was experiencing at the time, this type of product would definitely help to *Push It Along*. As the Universe would have it, the idea caught on, with other record labels using the technology for their major artists. One of the first to do it, was Goodie Mob for their second album *Still Standing*. Nevertheless, we were definitely the exception showing up at all of the open mic showcases.

I did all types of talent shows and auditions presenting that cd. The presentation was flawless, but the follow thru on the part of all the so-called Industry connects were another story. I even performed during the Lyricist Lounge tour that came to Atlanta with Reflection Eternal, which consisted of Talib Kweli and his partner Hi Tek. Tone, from Booth Research, performed at that same event with his group, Mass Influence, who were making major waves in the underground rap scene.

Back to Neal, along with all his other genius and talents, was the former manager of a group called Organized Konfusion, a while back. He always had his hand in something. I would sit at his crib out in Stone Mountain, while he, Big Rube from Dungeon Family fame, Lisa 'Left Eye' Lopes of TLC, and Professor Griff from Public Enemy would sit and build on deeper issues that impacted the world.

Around that time, Neal and Lisa were also scripting and pitching a film that they were trying to get distributed thru Sony pictures. They also had the help of Chuck D. Neal, who was always trying to help get me into the door, cast me as the supporting actor with Lisa. That's how I eventually met her and spent time building with her. She was a peculiar individual, yet very sweet and independent. She had this strong spirit about her and the firmest hand shake ever.

She also had a group of her own that she was working with called Jena Si Qua and Blaque. In between Lisa getting her artists out and Neal pitching the film, Lisa was going thru personal issues of her own, in which she became further and further distant, mentally and psychologically, until her untimely passing a few years later in Honduras. Neal tried to get me and Ralph to go with him and Lisa to Honduras, but we didn't make that last trip over there when she died.

That was a sad time for those that knew her and although I hadn't known her all that long or well, I was hurt by her passing, but not as much as Neal. The concept of the movie they were working on ended up getting 'jacked' and was launched in the form of a TV series called "Lost Angel."

Neal being Neal, moved onto his next idea of coming up with a way to sell music over the internet as opposed to in stores. I wasn't feeling that really. I didn't think enough people had computers to be doing all of that. He would always say that the music would soon only be available on the internet and we should jump on it now. It was like 1998 when he first mentioned this and wanted to get it started now with a project for me. I was more interested in getting a record deal, so a lot of what Neal had to offer I would be with for a second, but after an idea is in limbo for a minute, I'm moving on.

All of his ideas, and especially that one, would prove to be on the money. However, with no money to implement these ideas, we were stuck with no way to take advantage of these ideas. That Neal, man…, I love him to death! We have always remained close and he still serves as a constant advisor and supporter.

I spent a year or so of recording, recording, and recording…following one false opportunity after another. In the midst of recording, I did a lot of networking and trying to find my way into any industry event. At the time, I was building a song catalog and working towards getting better at songwriting. I was still driven, refusing to take No for an answer.

That same drive led me to being featured on a DJ Juice mixtape, which was huge at the time. New York DJs controlled the movement of the culture, with exclusive releases from top New York DJs such as Kid Capri, Ron G, Clue, Doo Wop, and S&S, to name a few. Juice was also a top tier DJ whose mixtapes circulated everywhere and could be copped at any discount mall or flea market, even on the streets. I performed hard hitting bars over a medley of instrumentals. By far, this was the best recording I had under my belt. Hearing my voice over those instrumentals on a DJ Juice mixtape, made me feel validated. I was making progress and could feel some momentum. All I had to do was just keep pushing. There was bound to be a Yes coming soon. But first, a few more Maybes.

Nas Platinum Party at Atlanta Live.   MR and Monkee (Pooh),

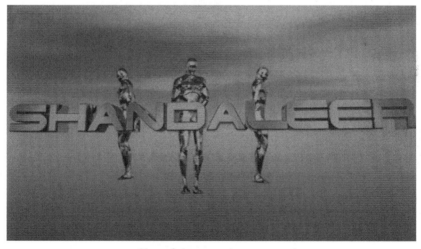

Shandaleer project artwork.

Scenario

One particular opportunity came in the form of a label called Noontime. I was introduced to them by a guy named Smooth. He was just that! Very charismatic, social, great talk game, and loaded with money! Somehow, Al and Larry met him while washing the J30 at the car wash and played my music for him. He liked it and wanted me to sign to him.

He immediately took me under his wing and had me temporarily posted up with him in a loft downtown Atlanta. On any given Sunday, you could catch us at Lenox Mall stunting, riding through the city in his candy apple red BMW or in the all-white drop top Benz. This guy was loaded with money and I didn't know where it was coming from.

At the time, Noontime was run by a guy named Nooney and they had a few hot producers that were making a name for themselves: J Dub, Anthony Dent, and newcomer Jazze Pha. I was actually in the studio when Anthony Dent played the track, he submitted for Jay Z and Too Short off of his second album *In My Lifetime, vol 1*. The track actually ended up getting placed on the album.

Noontime also had a R&B group named Absolut that they had just inked a deal with thru Def Jam. This appeared to be the perfect situation. I, of course, brought a recuperated Ralph (he'll explain in his book later), into the equation as my producer, which ended up being a crazy *Scenario* in itself. It just so happens that they were in a couple of meetings with the very same people that Ralph had bad business dealings with before when he was producing for a group out of Miami called Zoe Pound.

Now those guys were official. One of the guys from the group name Redd Eyez was real cool with Ralph and would come over to the crib from time to time, but most of the time, Ralph would be with them doing God knows what. Anybody who's somebody knows who they are, especially in the streets of Miami, Florida.

Anyway, the meeting was centered around a young artist named Nivea at that time, whom Ralph had done a lot of work with under that same situation. Ironically, we happened to be at this impromptu meeting, which was very awkward with a couple of lawyers and thugs turned music execs at a round table styled event.

Long story short, nothing came out of that opportunity, for various street and lawful reasons known and unknown to this day. To top it all off, they had wanted me to debut as an artist 6-8 years younger than I actually was. They had heard a song that I did with Khari, who was about the same build and complexion as me, was blown away by our chemistry, and wanted us to be the youngest duo out with this fabricated plan of theirs.

They also had this outlandish image that they wanted me to portray, with a plan of execution that I was simply not feeling at all! My whole thing was, "I ain't finna have homies clowning me back at the crib for lying bout my age and stuntin like I got it, when I don't...hell naw, I ain"t doing it!" Besides, that was the only song Khari and I collaborated on... we were both not with it!

MISTER

Don't get me wrong, the song, which was called, "1 Need Rest", was a smash actually, but we both rolled with two different camps and was moving in different directions. At that time, I didn't know a thing about the music BUSINESS and only wanted to be ME and do MY music. This was definitely not the machine to do that with. So, with that said, I didn't sign that contract either, which I think bothered Smooth and things started changing between us after that!

Smooth was a very cool dude and hung out with us on the regular, until one day he just disappeared. No more phone calls, nothing. All I remember is him asking to borrow my homie Al's laptop and was never heard from again. I happened to see Smooth again years later...we'll get to that part soon enough.

Larry stumbled upon another *Scenario* with some guy that had a studio, who was looking for artists. He told me about that guy and setup a time to go meet with him. At the time, I had no idea of what part of town he lived in...all I remember was that it was far. When we finally arrived, we found that he had a studio setup in his home. We went thru the garage entrance of his house and went downstairs into this room that had been turned into a studio lounge area.

It was nice! It had carpet and a couple of couches, with a restroom and the whole nine. Straight to the back, it was another room that had studio equipment in it. It had a door leading to the room with a huge console and speakers. To the left of the studio was the booth, where a nice recording microphone was there waiting. I was too excited about that...a real studio!

I know he gave us his name, but I couldn't remember it. All I remember was him saying that he knew Da Brat and that she was a good friend of his. He said that the dog, which was walking around chilling with us, was actually her dog and that he watches him for her when she's out of town. I'm like, "yea, yea, yea dude." I wasn't buying it one bit. Besides, with all the nonsense we had been going thru in Atlanta, I'd had enough with all the hoopla in this city. He even played us some records that he had of Da Brat's artist, a guy named 22. The records were pretty polished, but I wasn't that impressed or believed that even this 22 guy had anything to do with Da Brat.

Interestingly enough, the guy didn't want to do any producing for us or sign us at all. He mainly was offering us the opportunity to record in his studio at a certain rate per hour and promised that he would get the music to Da Brat, which could lead to another opportunity. I wasn't trying to hear the empty promise or the price he had for renting the studio time. Besides that, this guy was all the way on the other side of town! Needless to say, we didn't do any business with him.

A couple of years had gone by with disappointment after disappointment. Al had become "married with children" and officially off the scene. Larry was "everywhere" the party and ladies were, but it seemed to be a form of networking that kept him in the mix in Atlanta, helping him become a familiar face. Ralph had relocated to Little Haiti, Miami with Zoe Pound doing music as their producer. I had resorted to working odd jobs here and there, still working part time at MCI, also selling weed, and laying up with a Jamaican chick that put me onto different money schemes.

MISTER

The shift to wanting to make money out in the streets started to become the focus, because without money, moves were limited. You can't look the part, or get into certain clubs, or be available when opportunity knocks, with no money or time invested in the game. The whole process was frustrating. I seemed to be losing a little steam with this whole music thing.

I eventually, split from my Jamaican chick and hooked up with a girl who would become the mother of my child and we named our daughter "Genesis Lyric", which stood for "my beginning or first melody." At this point, music was the furthest thing from my mind as something that is going to bring home the bacon. Yet and still, I wrote and recorded every chance I got, however, the pursuit of it was out of the question. It was definitely "jobby job" time. Sometimes, 2-3 jobs at the same time. From delivery jobs, sales jobs, to collections jobs…you name it, I did it, to support my child and her mother.

I would still hit the city from time to time to hang out with friends and attend a few open mics and crush a few ciphers just to see if I still had it, but nothing major. For a while, even before I had my daughter, I was hanging with a new dude I befriended from D.C. named Rock "Solid".

Now, Rock was a very animated individual. In that I mean, he was always somewhere making his presence known when he was around. I remember when we first moved to Atlanta and used to catch the Marta back and forth to work, this guy was always around talking…loud! I used to think, like "damn, how I keep running into this n***a?" Everywhere we were, from the barber shop, to the Marta, to finally, at work…he was there.

It's funny how things work out, because I never could've imagine myself clicking up with dude, but as chance would have it, we did. He ended up getting a job up there at Booth Research, where I was working at. It only took a few lunch and smoke breaks before we finally hit it off. The story that we had on the first night of us hanging together is something I won't divulge in this book…let's just say we hooked up with two chicks for an interesting night of events.

While riding out that day, I found out he could spit and everything. Of course, that's all I need in common with most people in order to gel with them. So, after Krook and Pooh went back to VA, I held it down on my own, with Rock, who decided to hop on board and rep with me. We clicked up and started doing songs together under the name 7th Day, to keep the movement alive. I remember we use to frequent a spot called Studio Central (Mic Check Mondays, hosted by, Robert "Loki" Jenkins) that was downtown Atlanta up the street from the jailhouse.

Mic Check Mondays was a pure battleground. I would describe the cipher sessions down at FAMU, as boot camp in a sense. It trained me for moments like the ones I experienced at Studio Central. This venue was one of the first to host battle rap events. It was setup like a boxing match in the center of the space, with a rapper in each corner. There were three rounds, with different approaches each round. The first round was head-to-head over a beat provided by the DJ. The second round was acapella with no profanity. The third round was a performance, to show crowd participation and showmanship.

MISTER

This environment was insane, with rappers that repped cities from all across the country. I had been in Atlanta for two years so far, with no real opportunities to get on a stage anywhere. This was my chance to show up and show out. Now, besides rhyming against a few other rappers on campus, I never experienced organized competition. To my surprise, as someone who usually has stage fright, I approached the challenge as if it wasn't a challenge at all.

See, prior to Mic Check Mondays, and since the whole Shandaleer project and Noontime experience, I had been doing nothing but writing rhymes every day and freestyling to any beat within an ear shot. We would be at Cam's spot recording verses all day every day over all his beats. We recorded a few songs, but mostly we just <u>freestyled</u> rhymes for hours. These made for great "riding around" mixtapes to listen to, of just us.

Outside of Cam's homie, Fes Taylor, who was an artist from his hometown, it would be just me, Rock, and another homie, Kel, going for broke. The rappers at those battles had no idea of the practice we had been putting down already. Rhyming over instrumentals was nothing at all. This amount of confidence and the fact that I literally breathed rhymes, was the blueprint for victory after victory, taking out each rapper one by one. With each Win, my confidence was growing more and more. It was to the point tp where I felt that I couldn't lose. I was getting pulled to the outside to battle again, in the parking lot, the bathroom, huddled up in the corner before and after the events.

Everyone wanted to see how they would fare against the kid, and to keep it a "hunnid" there was some great talent that participated every week.

Dres the Beatnik was one of those guys. He was incredible with the beat box and could put on a show just by doing that alone, but from opening night to when it dissolved, my name was mentioned as one of the best there.

Every verse, was Mister this, 7th Day that. Not to mention I had crew with me that rhymed too! It would be me, Rock, Kel, my man Cam from Staten Island (crazy on the beats), and another guy I met thru Rock named Sheist from Brooklyn, NY. I had them all reppin 7th Day with me and each of us was winning battles. Of course, there had to be at least a couple of people that would test and pull out the best in me.

One night, a guy by the name of Fort Knox came up there straight going through rappers left and right. He was intimidating…built like he was fresh out of prison and a commanding voice. I recall being shook as hell in the back of the club watching dude, like "I hope I ain't battling this n***a tonight." There was absolutely no way to duck a battle like that when the entire building is screaming your name after every battle this guy is winning.

Eventually, the host got fed up and went away from the program to give the crowd what they wanted. Of course, the fan favorite would have to hold down his crown, which I did! He couldn't believe that I was freestyling by the way I was putting words together, especially when I did it in the acapella round where we couldn't curse or nothing! I would win that battle, but Fort Knox and I went on to have a few more monumental clashes. That's my guy right there…HEAVEE!

There was also a guy named 4Ize who I shared a few epic battles with there. He was known as a close friend and collaborator with radio host turned rapper, Ludacris. 4Ize was very charismatic, with a very unique style of rhyming and look for that matter. He wore glasses but would don an extra pair of glasses or goggles on stage. 4Ize had a very comical approach, in contrast to my aggressive and cynical battle style. We had some great battles.

After winning so many times, the host would allow me to just perform on the stage to open or close the event. To take advantage, I needed to come up with a song that could catch the crowd and I could start building an audience. It appeared to be just on time.

Cam had hooked me and Rock up with a track we went completely bananas on. Larry hooked up a studio session for us out in SW Atlanta, behind Greenbriar to record it. The song was called, "Lighter Fluid." It was basically, the both of us going back and forth with the hook only in the beginning and end of the song.

We would perform this song at Studio Central after every epic night of battling and had the crowd going wild. I remember when Pooh came back down to visit and saw how we had it popping in there. I wanted to make him and Krook proud that I was still keeping the 7th Day movement going. The crowd response felt good and that feeling of being on stage and having the people chant your name is something irreplaceable. It was a high that you never want to come off of.

That whole experience revamped my motivation to do something with my talent, but I was just too consumed by "real life" issues like job instability, no money, a failing relationship, and a newborn. If I could just get a little bit ahead on my bills, I could find the time to make something happen.

I would always hope for opportunity, which at this point, had turned to praying for an opportunity. Every night, before I went to bed, I would get on my knees and thank GOD for life, health, my family, and I would throw in a request to be blessed with an opportunity to do what I love most...my music:

"**Dear Lord Jesus, I thank you for waking me up this morning Lord**

Thank you for food, clothes, and for shelter Lord

I thank you for my daughter, and for her health Lord

I thank you for her mother and her health as well GOD

Please continue to look over us and keep your angels around us Lord

I pray for you to bless my mom and my dad

my brothers and sisters, nieces and nephews Lord

Continue to bless them with good health and protect them from all

harm Lord

I pray for all of those that are sick and locked down

And GOD, you know my heart, and really want you to just bless

me with the opportunity to do what I love most Lord

Bless me with the chance to be heard around the world and

show them the gift that you blessed me with GOD

Of course, I know that it is not MY will but YOUR will be done Lord I

pray that you protect me thru the night and allow me to awake in the

morning. It is in your son Jesus' name, I pray, AMEN"

Performing at Lyricist Lounge, held at Club Kaya

With Rock Solid and Pooh

Get A Hold

It's funny how sometimes you wonder if GOD is really listening to you, yet alone feel like granting your requests. In my opinion, that is where Faith comes in. If you have belief enough to speak to GOD in the first place, then that belief should go farther as to believe that GOD hears and will answer you. Now answers don't necessarily mean your wishes are granted, but every night I prayed that mine would be.

It was 2001 and I was about 7 years in on this journey of trying to make it Inside. The road was tough, full of plenty heartache and never-ending drama, both at home and in the streets. When you're pursuing something like this, you sacrifice a great deal, in which I sacrificed stability. I never had much consistency with keeping a job or a place to stay even.

Things were real now. I can no longer just live life sacrificing everything, being that I had a daughter now. It was a must to be able to provide for her. My child's mother was no picnic and stayed on me constantly about not being a deadbeat dad. It didn't matter, because that was something I refused to be anyway. Music or no Music, I wasn't willing to sacrifice my baby's future, she was my main responsibility and goal now. However, I still was determined to find a way to where I could still do both. So now, the goal of making it on the Inside, had company...let's get this Money.

I landed a job working as a delivery truck driver for Office Depot. It took the majority of my day, which was how I started to write songs in my head, because I couldn't write them while driving all day. I used to constantly listen to Frank Ski's Morning show with Wanda and Griff on V103.

Griff was a comedian/sports fanatic, who provided the show with all the sports updates and comic relief, alongside Wanda. He had the most distinct, irritating voice you can imagine, that I grew to get used to. He would always promote this comedy gong show night that he had at a spot called Café Red Train in Marietta, right where I was residing at the time. He would brag of celebrity guests and open mic competitions, with weekly prizes.

I had gotten so tired of the open mic and celebrity functions that Atlanta had to offer that I never paid it any attention. Before you know it, I was still working at Office Depot for about a year and a half, and found myself to be completely worn out with the daily routine of driving 200 miles a day, delivering product in these hick towns, 50 hours a week, and dead tired when I get off.

I would get home and fall asleep with my daughter in my lap, on the couch. I longed for Saturdays…to sleep in! That was one of the jobs that I, literally, walked out on. I was in the middle of loading my truck that morning. My baby momma had just dropped me off and we had gotten into it that morning. We were at a point in our relationship where I was working all the time, with never time enough to do things with her and the baby, or allow her time to do things without the baby, due to my work schedule.

Being that I was the only one working, I held down all of the expenses, so it wasn't much money left over to splurge on vacations, shopping, diamond ring, etc.… I was completely stressed over this whole period from pregnancy to birth, to infancy and struggling to *Get A Hold* on my situation.

My body was shutting down on me and I developed this illness called Vertigo, in which I found myself hospitalized and unable to walk without falling on my face. The closest example I can use to describe Vertigo, is the feeling you have trying to stand or walk after jumping off of a merry-go-round that was going extremely fast. Doctors say that it comes from stress. Wherever it comes from, it doesn't go away and can always be triggered to come back full swing. There is a prescription drug called, Meclizine, that I have to take for it. I still battle with it to this day.

My relationship at home was heading downhill and on this particular morning at the job, I was done with everything! I decided to just leave, get back in the car with my baby mama, and finish our argument, never to return to Office Depot.

You know, the "F*ck It" stage only stays in your system for so long, before reality bites again, especially after unemployment runs out. I was back to looking for another job and found one working at a collection agency called Nationwide Credit, in Kennesaw. How about that? I'm now working at a place that requires me to call and make people do something that I definitely wasn't doing at the time…pay their credit card debt!

I became cool with this younger cat in my training class, named Jermel aka Flick. We literally met on his birthday! He was originally from Detroit but relocated and graduated from school down in GA. Jermel was real cool, young but acted much older for his age. He was taking care of 3 kids, 2 of which was his girlfriend's, but make no mistake about it…they were HIS kids. He became one of my "job buddies" that I would hang with from time to time and get a ride from when my ride would break down, which was often.

That hanging would include a lot of cooking out, card playing, and smoking! I credit him for getting me well acquainted with the GA culture and a lot of their music. Thanks to him, I was put on to T.I. early, Yo Gotti, Three Six Mafia, T Rock, Project Pat, the list goes on. These were artists who I thought I would NEVER listen to, not to mention, actually like. The South wasn't running the game yet, so these artists were still on the come up. I met a lot of real street dudes from Marietta thru him, and they were cool peoples out there.

So, here I am at the collection agency every day, making phone calls and collecting money from accounts. I was really good at it and made a lot of money from bonuses and so forth. The only problem is that after a while, it becomes very demanding and redundant. Even though, I was making more money, it never seemed to be enough.

I still found myself clouded with expenses from childcare, car repair, utilities, you name it. Not to mention, the late and unpaid bills from the period of unemployment and the "F*ck It" stage came back to haunt me.

Eventually, we were evicted from our place and had to find emergency lodging in order to have a roof over our head. I can't tell you how many churches we hit up to assist us with rent and past due bills. Those resources were now exhausted, and things seem to be getting worse. Of course, I don't have to explain the status of my relationship at home. Honestly, it was rocky, but to give credit to my baby momma, she rolled with the punches we were given. Now she certainly wasn't quiet about it, but she stayed down…for the moment.

We would move from her mother's place to a hotel, from there to a friend's spot, then back to a weekly stay hotel. I was still working more and more hours, but somehow not making enough money to even get by. To top it all off, I was so busy being a "working man" that I forgot about my true passion, to make it 'behind the glass'. Something had to give…and fast!

MISTER

Holding my baby, Genesis Lyric…Everything Changed

Steppin' It Up

My man Larry, always had a gift for talking a good game. He's a natural charmer and a great illusionist. He could be broke as a joke and make you think he had ten stacks in his pocket. I say all of that to say, this very gift somehow talked us into recording at this studio he bought us time for, put a compilation album together, and get this...got us to headline with Wutang Clan at a major venue in Atlanta called Earthlink Live!

This was not your typical 'opening act' gig. We had two full dressing rooms right beside the WU, a catering service, the whole nine. There was no one else on the ticket but Wutang Clan and us!

Us, at this point, would be me, Pooh (Kallihan), his brother Dre (Gimmie II, producer and dope rapper) who had just got out of the military and moved to the ATL, Lou Don (monster producer straight out of VA...and crazy off the head rhymer, one of the young homies), Sup (also one of the younger homies, from VA), the homie/producer Cam, and Rock Solid. The event was so major that all our homies came down from VA to Atlanta for this.

We had a full bar worth of drinks from Henny, Goose, Coronas, juices. Not to mention, so much Haze and Kush in the air, where you couldn't help but inhale it if you simply breathed in the dressing room. It was crazy yo! Larry had really done it with this one! Of course, all of our significant others came out to watch the event as well. We were all donned in our VA Tech jerseys and rocked a full 30-min set. We had a blast!

After our set, we mingled with all the other members of the Wu…every last one of them, except Dirty who didn't make it of course. It was dope to witness one of the elite rap groups of all time perform on stage, from the side of the stage. Talk about being on the Inside! I soaked it all in, watching how they moved on stage, engaged with the crowd, and their group chemistry. This is the type of stuff you can't even pay for and I appreciated every moment of it.

The highlight was Method Man and his crazy theatrics on stage, but all in all, the whole Wu showed out that night…and so did 7th Day! The only missing link was Krook, who I know was proud as hell that we held it down for him! This whole experience really boosted my motivation to get back into this thing full swing. It was time to start *Steppin It Up*! I just didn't know where to turn.

I was still working at the collection agency, living out of my car, and spending money on weekly stays at different hotels with my daughter and her mother. It wasn't until after that Wutang show, and a month or so of growing agitated with my collection job, that Café Red Train and Griff popped up in my head.

I was just getting off work at 9pm, sitting in the 4 door Ford Escort hatchback that my great grandmother left for me when she died, and thinking about what was I going to do with my life? I had a trunk load of clothes in the back and decided to change right there in the parking lot, and head to Café Red Train.

Café Red Train was in a hood area of Marietta, on a street called Franklin Rd. Today, it is known as Franklin Gateway, that boasts a professional soccer facility, sports complex, renovated residences, businesses, and roads. That is now, but back then, Franklin Rd. was a street lined with apartment complexes, filled with nothing but Blacks and Mexicans! Every element of the hood could be found on Franklin, from drug selling, robbery, carjacking, to homicides.

The Red Train was in Franklin Plaza and was *the* hangout spot for every walk of life on Franklin and Marietta for that matter. I pulled up to a packed parking lot and didn't know what to expect. I walked up in the venue and immediately felt nervous. There was an Asian guy that greeted me at the door, by the name of Kevin, he would turn out to be the owner.

There were so many people piling up in there, the DJ's name was Cowboy, and he was spinning nothing but the top hits of the time. The venue had a sports bar feel to it. Soon as you came in, you walked down this huge corridor ramp where you could view the stage area to your left. Once you got all the way down, to your right, were the pool tables, the restrooms, and VIP area.

Once you made your way left towards the stage, you'd pass the bar, onto a floor filled with tables and seats. The far wall, stage right, resembled the Vietnam Wall in D.C. with nothing but celebrity framed pictures and signatures from all of them written directly onto the wall. I'm thinking to myself, "so here it is, the Red Train." Griff had spoken of this one rapper that had been winning his open mic competitions for a straight year on the air often. This one rapper's name was Que.

I noticed, simply off his entrance into the club, that it was him. Everybody spoke to him, he moved in a king like manner with a towel around his head. I'm thinking, "so this is the guy." You had to pay $5 to sign up and supply your own music instrumental or the DJ could play one, which I would soon find does not work to the advantage of the newcomers. I had gotten there so early that I was first on the list.

The concept of the Comedy Gong Show was this: Griff comes out and warms up the crowd with a brief comedy set, cracking jokes, and heckling the crowd…he introduces his celebrity guests, who would serve on a panel as judges…then he would introduce the guest comedian for the evening. After all of this, comes the Gong Show. Each artist has an opportunity to showcase their talent, whether it be singing, rapping, dancing, or comedy, and do so without getting gonged!

Usually, Griff or one of the celebrity judges would gauge the crowd's response and cut the artist's set noticeably short with a loud banging of the gong. This is completely setup to make you feel totally embarrassed and pride stricken, which should indirectly force you to 'step your game up'. Might I add that many have left the stage teary eyed and/or mad, ready to fight.

So here it was, my turn to perform. I step to the stage and Griff asks me my name, which I'm already sure is going to garner the butt of a few jokes. I tell him my name is "MISTER" from VA. After a couple of jokes about the name, he tells me to go ahead and do my thing…with the cord mic. He is the only one that keeps the cordless mic. I do a simple rap to let the crowd know that I can spit…didn't get gonged and actually got a good applause from the crowd.

I left the stage feeling real good about my performance, like maybe I could walk out of here with that $100. Yea right, sooner than later, it was Que's turn. I see how Que won so often…he was clearly the club favorite and he had a commanding, smooth voice as well. His style was similar to Biggie's with the flow and his freestyle was damn near flawless.

In the crowd this particular night, was a local artist that was making a lot of noise in the mainstream, named Archie Eversole. Archie had a hit single called "We Ready" that was a smash hit in the "A" and he was visiting on this night. He had a table with a bucket of Moet, and a couple of ladies in tow. He jumped up to spit something himself, after Que finished his set. For some reason, Que took this as an opportunity to challenge Archie. A head-to-head battle ensued between them, and though Archie gained a whole lot of respect from me as a down south artist coming off the head, Que shined as the crowd favorite that night.

After the battle, Archie had Que come over to his table to drink some Moet and exchange numbers, the whole nine. Griff kept praising Que all night and no one seemed to remember the "lil guy from VA" that killed it earlier that night. The whole time, I'm looking at Que like, "I want your spot homie…and I'm coming to get it." Being that I did more observing of him, than I knew he did of me, I had the advantage of sleeping on it and waiting for next Wednesday to try it again.

MISTER

Over the next six days, I would do nothing but practice freestyling about any and everything. I spent a lot of nights, up late, in our new place, an efficiency room at the All Round Suites in Marietta, writing rhymes and sparring this dude Que in my head. My baby momma would find me still up, sitting on the edge of the bed, like "what are you still doing up?"

I had nothing! I'm sitting there looking at my baby in a crib that sat right beside the queen-sized bed, which took up the whole room. I had to put a blanket over the crib, so the light from the TV wouldn't keep her awake. I just felt like a complete bum…I have a talent, time to use it!

Flyer for the Comedy Gong Show, hosted by Griff

MISTER

Enough!!

It was now a couple of days before Wednesday, and my anxiety was getting worse. I decided to let Jermel know that I was going up to the Red Train to battle some dude name Que, who had been winning. Over the days leading up to and on Wednesday, I kept telling him that I was really going to do it. He really didn't take me seriously, mainly because I didn't tell anybody at the job my outside ambitions or what my hobbies were. I'm kind of private when it comes to work and play.

He finally said he would come, but the main thing he kept saying was, "n***a, you better not be whack or I don't know you...fa real!" I'm thinking, "damn homie...it's like that?" Anyway, I promised to not disappoint him. The whole time, I'm praying I don't disappoint myself. I've always had the worst feelings of anxiety before an event and would always have this false sense of confidence to psych myself out. It's crazy, I know. Even as I'm typing this, I'm nervous all over again just reliving this whole event...literally, my fingers are shaking as I'm typing this.

Moving on, it was Wednesday and I was headed to the Red Train. I told my homie, Al, about it and he decided to fall thru and check me out himself. Besides, this was the only time I could get Al out of the house for a change. I told my other homies too, but for some reason they didn't have any belief in doing any open mic shows and after that Wutang Show, who could blame them. I had a whole different agenda and was in a situation where I had a sense of urgency to try anything at this point.

My man, Pooh, had just had a stroke, so he was bed ridden for a while. I know he would have loved to be there for this kind of action. I had to hold it down for the both of us, and our whole crew for that matter. So, here we are…me, Al, and Flick.

Again, I walked into the Red Train and Kevin, the Asian guy, was at the door taking money. The place was already packed, and no one really spoke to me, mainly because, no one remembered me! I go up to the DJ booth to sign up again with DJ Cowboy. Now, I had a cd on me with an instrumental of a track by my man Lou Don. Even though the track was hot, I wanted something more current to really rock the building.

Of course, if everyone heard a track that was familiar, it would give me an edge. Plus, I was going to freestyle everything, so I wanted something to "go off" on blazing! So, I ask DJ Cowboy if he has any instrumentals that I coulc use. He says, NO, and that it was not his responsibility to provide any of the artists music…I needed to bring my own. Wow!

Now, he must've forgot that I was just there last Wednesday and witnessed the barrage of instrumentals he threw on for Que, especially during the battle. I kept it humble and was like, "a'ight." I handed him my cd with the Lou Don instrumental on it. It was hot anyway, so it wasn't a total loss. My game plan was simple, I wasn't going to wait for my respect, I was here to take it. My sole purpose was to take this guy Que off the top block, not TRY to, but DO IT!

It was to the point where I had had *enough*! I was tired of being underestimated, sick of not being heard, and done with being humble! It was time that they got to see what was really going on…my time was *now*! Given all that emotion and drive, the reality was that underneath all of that bravado and attitude, was fear. I was prepared, but still even that didn't do anything to contain my anxiety attacks.

Flick kept checking up on me to make sure I was straight, but mainly, to see if I was really going to go thru with this…at least that's what I felt he was doing. Griff had a gig out of town on this particular night, so he wasn't there. He had a stand in, by the name of Nard, that hosted for the evening. Nard, was a comedian as well…very funny dude!

Anyhow, I don't even know what number I was on the list, but when it was my turn, I went up there and did my thing. Again, I introduced myself to Nard and the crowd as "MISTER" from VA. This time the jokes about the name came from Nard! After all of that, I did my thing on the mic. I spit over the instrumental I had and the crowd was cool. They had a look of content on their faces and I received a few smiles and cheers during and after the performance. The main thing is, I didn't get gonged!

Once I was done, Nard came up on the stage and told the crowd to give it up for me one more time. The 'give it up' claps I received, just wasn't enough for me and it pulled the competitor in me to the front. I grabbed the mic back from Nard, looked towards the back where my Respect was standing at and said, "thank y'all, but I really just came here tonight to battle Que." After that, I gave the mic back to Nard and immediately, you heard chatter and noise from the crowd, like "oooohhhhh-whhaaaatttt." I recall Nard saying, "whaaatt…this lil n***a got nutz!"

Everybody started laughing. I don't know if they were laughing at what Nard said, or the fact that this "lil n***a" is stupid if he thinks he's beating Que tonight! Flick was just happy that I didn't mess up on stage, so he was a go at this point, as far as rooting me on. The remaining artists on the list that night did their thing, but no one cared, because all everyone wanted to see was Que.

Nard decided not to let Que perform, but rather to "destroy this lil n***a real quick" while the judges deliberate. I ran into an old partner of mine in there named Malachi, who I used to run with when I first moved to Marietta in the old MoonRaker Apartments, off Delk Rd. He was with my other partner, Mo aka Mad Moe, from the old MoonRaker crew. Their whole crew was from Pontiac, Michigan. Moe had a deal with MC Breed a while back and they had relocated down to Atlanta and were working with Rumeal Robinson, who was a star at University of Michigan and NBA.

We hadn't seen each other in a few years, since back in the day, freestyling, smoking out, and chilling. Malachi was shocked to hear I was challenging Que. He was like, "Que is my man too." I was like, "hey, well ya man is about to get it tonight."

The moment of truth was approaching, so I went back up to DJ Cowboy and asked him, specifically for an instrumental to rhyme over. Again, he said he didn't have anything to give me and that I would have to just rhyme over whatever he got. I was too hot with him at this point but was like 'whatever'. The crowd was building up in anticipation and you could hear and see it. My anxiety was at a full time high, but so was my adrenaline!

MISTER

They called the both of us to the stage for the battle…finally, it's ShowTime! Standing on the stage, next to Que, he immediately appeared as a giant. Not only in physique, but in stature, because the whole crowd was chanting his name, people running up to him, dapping him up, yelling "kill this lil n***a." The whole scene, along with my emotions, almost to the exact pinpoint, I would relate to later in a movie called, 8 Mile. It was exactly like that!

He had his whole crew and I had, Flick and Al, who were both quiet as hell and just looking at me directly, as if to find some kind of confidence in my eyes. They were giving me looks of both actually…Al had a look of confidence in his friend, no matter what…but also with a look of "n***a, you better bring it!" Flick had a look of, "ok, this what you wanted…let's see what you do with it!" I know I had a look of sheer confidence, but inside, I was just numb.

I stood on the far side of the stage, by the wall and Que stood opposite of me, by the entrance of the stage…where the majority of his supporters and all onlookers stood. Nard stood in between us and before he could get anything started, I grabbed the mic and spoke to make sure there was no misunderstanding…after all, I'm outmanned in here. I simply said:

"I don't mean any disrespect, but I consider myself the best
So, in order for me to prove I'm the best, I have to beat the best
So, Respect my n*a"**

Both the crowd and Nard acknowledged the realness and sincerity in what I said, so the battle was good to go down without any ignorance popping off. In case it did, however, my man Flick had the backup in the car. With that said, it was time to get it on.

I had to go first, being the challenger and all. I decided to do a little something, just to show I could really rap. Now, I had prepared a few lines, but none of them popped up when it was time for me to rhyme. I can't even remember the WACK beat DJ Cowboy gave me, but I made it out alive and some cheers from the crowd. I think they were just cheering because I was finally done and Que could get to 'destroying me'.

As soon as it was his turn, the crowd went crazy…Cowboy hooked him up with the hottest instrumental at the time, "Pass the Courvoisier." Que straight went IN on me! I don't recall everything he said, but he clowned my signature dog tags, that I kept around my neck from my boot camp days. With every line he said, my confidence got lower and lower. The look on my face, had to be a look of uncertainty at this point and I was panicking on the inside, like "what the hell have I gotten myself into?"

It got worse…he said some line about "choppin off my head and sh*ttin down my neck." That line did it!! You couldn't even hear the rest of what he was saying from the crowd noise. People were at the base of the stage grabbing him, whooping, and hollering…pointing at me and laughing.

It was at this moment, that everything became slow motion to me. I could hear my heart beating, all around me, I'm looking at people going crazy, Nard shaking his head giggling, Cowboy laughing, the judges grinning, people slapping five to each other, the building was caving in on me. I look over at Al and Flick, they were submerged by the crowd of people that were all going crazy over the stupid rhymes they just heard and they had this look of 'damn…but, it's all good, you tried'. I looked at Que and noticed how he was soaking it all in. He had the 'I do this, I been here before' look in his face. Right then, I snapped out of it and didn't wait to be told, on whether or not, I could go again. They still had the same instrumental on, so I grabbed the mic, turned into a monster, and went IN! I don't remember much of what I spit, but I do remember the lines that changed the game:

"last week Archie told yo ass that you wasn't ready
Everything that I spit, get more spin than Pirelli"
(looked at the crowd, pointed at Que), "I'm bout to piss on dis n***a
like R.Kelly"

Now, that was one of the lines that I prepared from last week, remembering when Griff showed the footage of the R. Kelly porn tape on the big screen. It was very new and relevant, at that time. This meaning, no one had a chance to put it in a rhyme yet. In other words, perfect timing!

After that line, the crowd went into a frenzy! They were falling all over the place, looking back at Que, who had the stunned look on his face! Once I saw that, I officially had the eye of the tiger going…I even said a line or two about Cowboy's hairline, which was notoriously receding. That line got the crowd even more stupid and it felt good to get him back for dissing me with the track selection.

There was nothing Que could say, after I had finished, to redeem himself. Just like that, his fans became my fans…at least for the night. My two homies were the happiest dudes in the building, besides me! They both dapped me up, with excited hugs, along with the rest of the audience who now were highly interested in speaking to the "lil n*gga named MISTER from VA."

I remember getting love from so many people, but Que showed none at all. He didn't even speak to me afterwards, or maybe he tried, but it was too much going on. I don't recall seeing him after my verse was done.

I went back to my efficiency room at the All Around Suites, on the other side of Franklin Rd., by Dave n Buster's and told my baby moms what happened. She was real happy for me, and I was still elated. I sat on the edge of the bed, in the same spot where I was writing a week prior and just soaked it all in. The whole night was one to remember and I didn't want the feelings that I had to end.

I looked at my daughter, asleep in her crib, with the blanket draped over the side rail. I looked at her mother, who had gone back to sleep, and I looked at the room we were in. I sighed, knowing that we're still doing bad, but we're blessed to have a roof, some food, and each other. Besides, my emotions were still high from the events of the night and it would take more than that to discourage me right about now.

I thanked GOD for being with me in the Red Train, said my same prayer, and held onto my faith that GOD has more to come for me. I closed my eyes and relived the whole night over and over, until I fell asleep.

MISTER

Always reppin' 7th Day, with my signature dog tags from bootcamp.

My right-hand man, Jermel aka Big Flick

Rock Rock Y'all

The next day was back to normal. Reality placed me back at my cubicle at Nationwide Credit Services. There I was, after a night of pure elation and victory, back at my desk, placing calls to bad debtors. I was tired of hearing supervisors walking around, so called "motivating" everyone with 'let me hear you dunning, don't forget the mini Miranda, get out of typing, come on people put some money on the board!" Oh my GOD, if I can just fly away from here, I would!

At the job, they do this thing, whenever someone gets a huge payment, to get everyone's attention and announce their large payment. Every large payment is preceded with a supervisor yelling, "put em on hold, put em on hold…!" Hey, it's a big deal to get one of those announcements on the floor. I must admit, that I've been the recipient of a few of those announcements for outstanding performances.

On this particular day, though, there was the familiar "put em on hold, put em on hold…we want to acknowledge Mister today, he won the competition last night at the Red Train by beating the reigning champ!" I was shocked!! I couldn't believe that anyone even knew, because I didn't say anything to anybody. Immediately, I looked across the floor and saw my man, Flick, grinning! Right then, I knew he told it!

I wasn't mad at all though…at least I got his respect for knowing how I get down on the mic now. All of the anxiety was building back up now, because I had to go back on Wednesday and do it again. This time, I had more people from the job coming out, wanting to see if "Mister" is really all that good. I told my homies about it too and hyped it up to them, about how the Red Train is a spot we need to take over.

Pooh was still in bed rest, so he couldn't get out. I went over to his crib to tell him what happened and everything. He was happy, but not really interested in anything else, except getting his health back and who could blame him. I was missing the homie out here in the streets with me. This was actually the first time that I was really going at it alone.

On the days leading up to the next Wednesday, word was spreading around a whole lot. A couple of other coworkers would invite me over to their cribs to just chill and, of course, rhyme. I had a partner named Solo, who had a video camera and he vowed to bring it on Wednesday to get some footage. This made me even more nervous for some reason. It was now that time again.

I had been listening to the radio and heard Griff announce another night of competition at the Red Train. He had missed the previous week and the happenings that went down, so he was anticipating what was to come tonight. He wasn't the only one, I was too! I arrived to the Train with a few of the homies and sat in the car for a minute, to get right (hint).

The parking lot was extremely packed, as usual, and I was a nervous wreck…again! Once I got inside, again, Kevin was at the door taking the money. You could tell he was enjoying the success of his club. Kevin is *the* Asian of Franklin Rd., who had stood the test of time with his spot. Everyone loves Kevin and no one has ever tried to get over or rob him, which is odd, given the area his club is located in. Now that I think about it, it wasn't odd, because Kevin was no push over and usually hired "hood" hands to assist him in the club, to make sure he was straight, goons like my homie Mad Moe, for instance.

Anyhow, after I paid to get in, YES, I paid to get in...I was still a newcomer in there, so no perks. I paid to get in, then proceeded to the DJ booth to sign up. I knew it was going to be a problem before I even got up there to speak to Cowboy, being that he was on that B.S. last week with the instrumentals.

I forgot about the diss I gave him during the battle, but he didn't! As soon as I got up there to sign up, he went in! I tried to act like nothing happened, with a smile on my face, thinking we'd moved on from the nonsense of last week. I'm thinking I'd earned his respect now, by doing my thing and he would show more love...I was wrong! Immediately, he goes off with "n*gga, I don't appreciate that sh*t you did last week on that mic...I don't care if you won or not, it don't mean sh*t to me!"

I jumped in at this point, like "hey, I did what I had to do...I felt you was disrespecting me by telling me you didn't have any instrumentals, then you go and play a whole gang of them once Que got on stage, now *that* was some bullsh*t!" We then engaged in a back and forth, yelling in the ear match, over the loud music, with a bunch of "I'm a grown a** man talk!" Hilarious...at least now!

We ended up coming to an understanding, with me apologizing for the route I took in handling the situation, and him telling me, "it was a good one, though…you killed it." He also explained that it was nothing personal, it's just the politics of the game. You have to earn those types of perks with the DJ. He went on to laugh about the joke I did of his hairline and he was a great sport about it.

GOD totally has a sense of humor, because I certainly rock a baldie today. Yep, be careful what you say about people. My mother taught me that a long time ago. Anyhow, we dapped each other up and he said that he would make sure he had some good instrumentals for me…mission accomplished!

The scene was completely packed! There was about 10 or so, people from my job that came to support me, including my new fan, Flick! In addition to him, Rock Solid, Dre, Sheed, Seven, and Larry came out to see what this Red Train thing was all about. The baby momma got her mother to watch Genesis, so she could come out as well. I'm sure her objective was the same as Flick's the previous week, to see if I really was doing my thing at the Red Train.

The celebrity guests for the night, was an up-and-coming comedian by the name of Bubba. This guy was hilarious! He wore this funny, top hat that resembled Busta Rhymes' hat he used to wear when he first came out. The other celeb was Darius Rucker, aka, the black guy from Hootie & the Blowfish. This guy had sold millions and millions of records, known all around the world, and he was in the Red Train on Franklin Rd. tonight!

He was there promoting his solo album that he had coming out on Hidden Beach Records. This was a new label rumored as the one Michael Jordan had backed, and it had artists such as Jill Scott, Jazzy Jeff, and Darius Rucker. The other celeb there that night, was Brian Cox, who was fresh off a Super Bowl win with the New England Patriots. I was a fan of Brian Cox, since he played with my favorite team, the Miami Dolphins. I was amazed that this NFL great, who was known all around the world, fresh from the Super Bowl, was at Café Red Train, on Franklin Rd.!

It was then, that I noticed Griff had a lot of pull within the industry of sports and music entertainment. Between the celebrity guests and the host of supporters that came to watch me perform, I was completely stoked and nervous as hell! I strayed away often, going way across the venue to a corner to sit by myself. I would pace back and forth, between friends and the bar. When I'm feeling like this, I can't drink, stand, or sit still. It is extremely one of the most irritable moments that I have in my life. Again, even now, I'm typing with my hands shaking…just reliving the moment, it's crazy!

I had a few people that remembered me from last week, mainly the rappers. One, in particular, was named Baby Boi. He congratulated me on the battle I won last week. He said Que was his boy, but I got him fair and square. I thanked dude for the compliment and asked if he rhymed too. He said, yea, and that he would be rapping tonight. We dapped and I left him with a 'good luck' remark and that was that.

The night was getting ready to start, but finally I noticed and thought to myself, "where's Que?" I didn't give myself that much credit as to TOTALLY destroying the guy. I just knew he was coming back tonight, to do it again. A part of me, no, let me rephrase that, ALL of me was happy that he didn't show up! I felt a total sigh of relief and just knew that if he didn't show up, tonight was just going to be a night of fun and good stage performances, certainly I didn't foresee what was about to happen.

My man, Malachi, was in the building again, who always made you feel special once he spotted you, "Yooooo Son, what's the deal Son?!" He remembered the battle from last week and wanted to check me out again. Most people didn't know that when I first moved to Atlanta, I met Malachi out here in Marietta at an old apartment complex called MoonRaker. We used to freestyle back then all the time, but his verses were extremely polished! Put it like this, I was surprised HE wasn't in these battles, taking all the money and I was surely hoping that he wasn't trying to have any bright ideas now.

Anyway, the performances finally started going down and soon it was my turn to rock. Griff came me a special introduction as the "new lil guy named MISTER from VA" that he heard beat Que last week. He, personally, wanted to see me do my thing since our first meeting when I came. This time I had the honor of getting HIS mic, the cordless one, to do my thing.

I remember it vividly…I was wearing a VA Tech Hokies jersey, the one I wore at the Wutang show we did a few months ago. I had my hair braided, but with a do-rag on and a VA hat that matched the jersey! I had on a pair of triple-5 cargo pants and a semi-fresh pair of orange timberlands on my feet. I was orange and burgundy down, reppin hard! I also had my signature dog tags around my neck, that I kept ever since I left boot camp and I even had orange wristbands on…yep, I looked like a rapper!

Once I grabbed the mic, all the anxiety rush was gone and it was ShowTime once again! I thanked all my peoples for coming out to support and told DJ Cowboy to drop the beat. Even though, we peaced everything up earlier, I still had brought my own instrumental to rock over. I used a beat from my man, Lou Don. Once it came on, I went into a hot 16 that immediately had the crowd in a frenzy...after that verse, I went to my "crowd participation" hook, but I definitely wasn't going to be on no "*Rock Rock Yall*" chants. I kept it all the way VA and repped my team:

"when I say Seventh, yall say Day...c'mon Seventh, (Day), Seventh (Day)
when I say dat Boy Don't, yall say Play...dat Boy Don't (Play), that Boy Don't (Play)"

After that, I went to a second verse of straight freestyle! I rapped about everybody and everything that I saw in front of me! I find delight and throwing people's names in my raps and watching their reaction, like "he said my name in that joint...ahhh!" It's cool stuff for a freestyler to see. Flick, was in rare form and Super Crunk...getting bent off nothing but Heinekens and Red Stripes.

I'm not exaggerating when I say that everyone was on their feet. After I finished, Griff congratulated me like no other. It felt great to get praises from the top heckler host of the evening. My turn was over, and it was cool to get praises and hugs from everyone. I was thinking, cool, no battling, just a good performance...I can chill and have a good time for the rest of the night and collect my money (of course, that's still the reason I'm here in the first place, remember).

I can't remember how much time lapsed or how many performers had gone by, before I was "called out" by one of the performers. I was in the back by the pool tables and was barely paying attention to the guy on stage rapping, at least until, I heard my name come out of his mouth. So, there it is, a challenger already and it just so happened to be the same guy who I chopped it up with earlier and gave dap to, Baby Boi!

This guy, after showing me love all night, goes up on stage and disses me in his freestyle rap. Now, Baby Boi, is a phenomenal freestyler! His performance is all freestyle, no hooks, no breaks, just 5 minutes of 'going in'. He was a marine that used to spend his spare time coming to town, looking for battles. Of course, I found out all of this later. He was stocky built and wore a ball cap on real low. He was a bit like me, which kind of scared me, in the fact that he was a humble dude, but totally arrogant and disrespectful on that stage.

So, he calls me out in his rhyme and all I can see is my peoples looking for me to "get that n*gga". Griff grabbed the mic afterwards and announced that, while the judges decided who won the cash, MISTER and Baby Boi will square off! I'm laughing, dapping my people up, letting them know "I'm bout to destroy this dude", showing all the confidence in the world. Inside, frightened.

"And the New!" Red Train reigning champ, Mister from VA (that's

LA.com behind me)

The "SD" stands for Seventh Day…free Mike Lundy (on shirt)

Rumble in The Jungle

All that anxiety that went away earlier, was back on full steam! I tried to play it off so bad, by assuring my peoples that it was all good, "I got this, don't worry." I wasn't so confident inside though. What if this guy steals my glory before I even have a chance to revel in it for another week? Could this be karma that quick, for me to feel the same way I made Que feel last week? It can't be! It won't be!

We both got up on the stage and I mean, it was packed in the Train! It was damn near standing room only, if it wasn't for the tables in the front of the stage. Being that my coworker, Solo, had filmed this whole night, and I watched this footage over a million times, I can actually tell the story from both an outside viewer perception and as a participant.

Baby Boi was given the chance to go first, which I definitely didn't oppose to…gives me time to conjure up some quick lines (battle secret). DJ Cowboy gave Baby Boi a monster track too, the same one I roasted Que on last week, Busta Rhymes "Pass The Courvoisier" beat and he went in! He went completely hard and the crowd was showing him much love with the oooohs and ahhhhs! I started pumping myself up, by literally, hitting my chest! I was whimping up inside after every hard line and I had to get the "hoe" out my system…like, fa real.

I tried to think of some lines, but couldn't because I was too caught up in the crowd's reaction to his rhymes. All I could do, was start praying that I give it my all to beat this dude. Finally, his turn was over and it was time! DJ

Cowboy threw on the Mr. Cheeks "Lights Camera Action" beat. As soon as I grabbed the mic, the crowd started screaming, as if this is what they were waiting for. Let me tell you, it's something about having 'home-court advantage', in this case, people that believe in you. It will bring things out of you that YOU wouldn't even believe you had in you.

That quickly, all of the anxiety, and chump syndromes I was having, was gone! Before I started rapping, Flick had passed me a bottle of Red Stripe to sip on, to calm my nerves. It did nothing but keep my mouth wet and gave me something to hold onto while I rapped. Every rapper knows, we need something in our other hand while rhyming…a bottled water, drink, towel, something to hold. If we don't have nothing at all, we grab the crotch of our pants.

The beat dropped and I immediately went into spittin' a pure 'off da head' flow…riding the beat perfectly with wordy sentences that had the comedian, Bubba, losing his mind! Baby Boi messed up by moving with me on stage in the same rhythmic fashion that I was, while I was backing him up! It was as if, HE was even feeling the flow. I ended the verse with:

"…you aint ready for this, microphone supremacist, microphone analyst, microphone terrorist, n***a, I'm tryin to see why you came, why Red Train you better off dancing at Blue Flame…"

The crowd went wild with that one! I just rapped the whole time with no major punchlines or nothing, because I couldn't think of any while he was rhyming…then all of a sudden, something popped up in my head for those last two bars and it was right on time. Baby Boi couldn't wait to grab the mic again and come back. I, on the other hand, was feeling somewhat relieved that I got through the first round respectfully, though not convincing enough, at least in my eyes AND Baby Boi's!

Cowboy gave him Biggie's "One More Chance" beat, the remix one…very mellow. It didn't seem to matter to Baby Boi though, because he went in on me. He started out hot, straight killing me with just what seemed to be a flawless flow, no lie. I started to get nervous again, because it was killing me that I couldn't think of anything while he was rhyming. I could see Griff motioning to Darius and Brian Cox, that he had his money on me, which made me even more nervous.

Meanwhile, Baby Boi was clowning me from head to toe! All kinds of Halloween jokes, from all the orange I had on…short jokes, dog tag jokes, "you soft" jokes…you name it. The crowd was feeling him on a few lines too, to the point where I really needed to pull something out on my next turn.

It was at that moment, that I thought of my man Krook, who was locked down and I just thought how much he would have wanted to be here, killing it onstage. My dude is in a box, doing a life bid, and this was his dream too. I felt I needed to rep for him, and for all my VA crew for that matter. We came too far from home to make something out of nothing and I felt that the guys I was raised around were the hardest dudes in the world, by far. I used to rhyme in the projects for gangstas with nothing but guns, dope, and fiends all around. Those dudes used to say that I needed to be doing something with this rap.

I thought of all that while on that stage in that moment. Right then, I looked towards my homies who were all posted together in the cut, watching the whole thing, and I pointed at them and said, "I'm a do this for yall." With that said, I really felt at that particular time, that I couldn't lose…it ain't a person alive that can see me on this mic right now! I quickly noticed that Baby Boi was losing steam and the crowd was more anticipating my next turn, than getting more into the jokes he was putting out there on me.

It was now my turn again, and Cowboy gave me one of my favorite beats, the Cash Money joint "Still Fly". I mean, the beat straight sounded like a 'victory' track at this point. Soon as it dropped, I felt on top of the world, like I won already.

The crowd just wanted a show at this point. The whole crowd was out of their seats and all at the front of the stage now, including my man Flick, my baby moms and her friends, my man Malachi was standing by me, Griff was right beside us on stage. I remember his leg was hurt from some accident, so he was hobbling around all night up there.

When the beat dropped, I was too hype, like "oh,oh,oh,oh" and said the words that described my whole feeling, pointing at Baby Boi, "ain't no competition in here man, ain't no competition", while grinning from ear to ear. I let all the arrogance that my man Krook was known for, aggression that the homie Pooh had, the attitude of my hometown, and FAMU

ciphering out, which changed me from the "lil humble guy" to the most
disrespectful emcee on the planet.

I straight aimed to embarrass this guy now for having the audacity to
call me out, especially after showing me love…yep, I was in that mode! This
entire sequence was recorded by Solo, but in an effort to transfer it from
analog to digital, I gave it to Neal to handle. One of the biggest misfortunes
ever, is him losing my tape during a move. I'm still hurt by that, because this
particular night, was one of the best moments of my entire lifetime. Before
losing it, I had the chance to view it numerous times, so the memory is still
very vivid enough for me to recount the verse I delivered, line by line:

"n***a you speed rolling down a dark road with no head lights
I'll whoop ya a** till it's lookin like a Red Stripe (in my hand)
You ain't ready for styles, comin off da noggin
N***a, I'll whoop ya a** straight up, no problem
N***a, the Red Train is MY f ----g establishment
It's where I battle kids, I'll send you home to your mommy crying on
some tattle sh—
You can't handle this, you can't see da man coming straight off da head
with this
The microphone analyst, yo ask the panelists (pointing at the judges)
They know I got in your d—n sh--, you d—n b -- h
Betta step off da stage with dat weak s**t, peep s**t
Me and my n****z we in here, on some deep sh—
f—k around and get your neck broke, n***a you this close I
hang yo a** off with a rope, n***a you misquote

N***a sticking up for Que, is that yo b---h?

I whooped dat n***a a** last week, you need to git, skip, scatter n***a

(the crowd is out of control right about now…all over the place, Griff is having security to try and keep people back from the stage…it's wild)

Told u my rhymes off the platter n***a,

You shoulda known betta to come and try to battle n***a

It's all over, Malachi you betta get him (pointed at Malachi)

That n***a right there is my dog, yo f--- n sic em

(crowd goes crazy again after every line right about now, mainly because that last line was said as I watched Malachi try to grab Baby Boi, like 'you finished')

Get this n***a off my lawn, somebody betta tell this n***a poof be gone,

N***a's retarded! Why da f—k you wanna test this

Da microphone nexus, n****z can't create da connection

I'm on some next sh--, word to Cowboy I'll ride you like a saddle

Cuz n****z ain't ready to battle, you going upstream without a f----n paddle

Yo s**t churned, simple muhf****n when will they ever learn

Keep playin with that fire, yo a** gon get burned

(now he makes the mistake of trying to reach for the mic and Griff quickly tries to intercede before I address it)

MISTER

n***a you ain't got no more turns, n***a it's over,

the microphone soldier, yo f ---r I told ya

I'm walking away with a hundred bucks n***a, I sold ya

(Griff hobbles off screaming, along with a crowd that has totally overtaken security and bumb-rushed the stage and ME)

Get yo a** off da f----n stage, b -- h" - *and that was that!*

I was then rushed by what seemed to be the whole club, like "it's over, it's over!" I felt like Muhammad Ali at the conclusion of his fight against George Foreman. This definitely was my *Rumble In The Jungle* moment.

Baby Boi couldn't do nothing but show love AFTER everything was calmed down, of course. I have to admit, I totally lost myself in that one and went all out! Bottom line is, I won! Afterwards, I went over to meet Darius Rucker and Brian Cox, who both congratulated me and showered me with 'good nothings' in my ear all night. Darius gave me his personal number to call him, because he wanted to get some music from me to present to his label, Hidden Beach Records.

For the rest of the night, it was nothing but picture taking, hand shaking, fun and I went home with my $100, minus $20 that I spent in the club of course, hey we was balling that night! It felt good to have another week of accomplishment under my belt.

In 3 weeks, I had popped my cherry at the Red Train, took on the King of the venue, beat him, then took on another worthy challenger, and beat him. I met one of the top selling artists in the music industry and got his personal number, to possibly having an opportunity to get a record contract.

I met a famous football player, who both my Dad and I watched on Sundays, and got a chance to look at a REAL Super Bowl Ring up close! Hey, that's a big deal to me. To top it off, one of the city's top radio personalities was vouching for me. I really felt blessed at this point and felt that GOD was finally answering my prayers to get Inside the music industry. I'm too excited about what's to come!

MISTER

Money Maker

The very next Wednesday turned out to be totally different than the previous weeks. Usually, the Gong Show comprises of talent that perform throughout the night for celebrity judges, then someone goes home with $100. The battles just happen to take place impromptu, they're not planned at all.

On this particular Wednesday, Griff decides to forego the usual proceedings of the Gong Show and decides to change it up a bit. He gets on the stage and says that it will not be a Gong Show tonight, there is no list, so whoever came to perform, come back next week. He then said, "MISTER come to the stage please." I'm puzzled, like what is this all about.

Mind you, I had an even bigger following that came out to support tonight, so they all just wanted to see me perform anyway and leave. On a side note, let's remember that the Red Train, is a bar on Franklin Rd, (the hood) in Marietta, GA, about 15-20 minutes from the city. This spot, on a Wednesday, opened at 8pm and didn't close until 4:30 am…packed the whole time! Griff had this spot jumping with all of the connects and promotions from radio.

Back to the matter at hand, Griff calls me to the stage. I had on some black jeans, a white shirt, and a headband that had "MR." on one side and "7th Day" on the other side. I had a black fitted cap and do-rag over the braids, of course. Ok, so now I'm up on stage…now what? Griff has me stand to the far end of the stage, by the wall. He then says, "I want everybody in here who thinks that they can beat MISTER, to this end of the stage." I'm like, "what?!"

So now, there is a line of emcees on the entry side of the stage, ready to come up one by one to battle me. Amongst all these emcees, were the two dethroned ones, Que and Baby Boi. So now, they're back for more and this time, I know they came prepared. I, on the other hand, was not prepared for this whatsoever. Griff set it up for me to rhyme first and then everyone else would follow.

I was not in the mood to battle a club full of emcees and it quickly showed. I did my verse and dissed "no one" in it. I just did my usual cocky, confident flow and dazzled the crowd with the freestyles. Got my usual screams, ooohhhs, and ahhhhss, done! Que came up next and went IN!

It didn't work to his benefit, however, because it came off more angry and bitter than confident. He hit well below the belt talking about my baby mother in the crowd and everything. During the infamous Nas and Jay Z battle, after the effects of what Nas did with "Ether", Jay released "Super Ugly." That song is what comes to mind, when I recall Que's verse. The crowd started booing him…he got mad and left, the CLUB!

This would be the same result for mostly everyone else that came up to battle. They were coming up with rhymes that you know they wrote specifically for me. Guys I hadn't seen ever in my life, were coming onstage, like "this for that b*tch a** n*gga MISTER, I don't know you but here it is!"

The situation got ugly, because Griff wouldn't allow me to rhyme after each one of them, he wanted me to wait until the end to go up again, after all of them were done. It was crazy! I had my whole crew with me on one side of the club and all of the rest of the competitors and their peoples were on the other side. Griff and security had to intervene a few times, because between my people that I had with me and the opposing peoples, were screaming out deadly threats and ready to fight after each disrespectful line.

The only problem for all those guys and good thing for me, was that they were all WHACK! There really wasn't a need for me to respond, because the crowd was booing them off of the stage! They would get mad, cuss the crowd out, Griff would crack jokes on them, they would threaten Griff, threaten me, and head outside! I honestly, wasn't trippin' off none of it, because I was deep in there, plus my man Flick was strapped and wouldn't leave my side for nothing!

I finally went back up and went round for round with one of the guys who did stand the test of time on stage and ripped it! His name was Remo, from a crew called 5th Nation! They were deep too, and Remo was a monster on the mic!

He was originally from New York or something and could really go in with the lyrics. I definitely saw him as a problem. We went for about 4 or 5 rounds, before the crowd and Griff had heard enough, and claimed me as the victor. I could see it in Remo's eyes though, that he wasn't impressed, and I wasn't either. We both got each other's respect that night, and we never battled again, except with songs and performances. He held his own, but I was the crowd favorite who would never experience a loss in the Red Train...period!

It was official now; I was *the* reigning King of the Red Train and the talk of Marietta! Week after week, I would meet celebrity after celebrity coming up there to judge and see me destroy emcees on the mic, with crazy 'off the head' performances. Griff would do this thing where he tells me what to rap about and what to include, then I just go in. It wasn't long before I started experiencing real 'groupie' action from the Train.

Everyone knew I was with my baby mother, who faithfully showed up there weekly, but that didn't stop the females from going hard. On top of female groupies, you have male groupies too. They just want to hang, buy you a drink or two, throw you some green, you know the "let me know if you need anything, I gotchu n*gga", who I don't even know their names.

Make no mistake about it, there was a lot of genuine love I was getting, but it was a must to stay alert. Some of that love is an extortion waiting to happen. It's funny, you can tell the real from the fake ones though. I stayed with my crew, or to myself.

The Red Train was steady poppin' with me being the 4th face of it, behind Kevin, Griff, and Cowboy. Being the best rapper in the building, ended up being a huge *Money Maker* for me. Any contest that went down, I won it. I paid my weekly rent at the extended stay with the money from Red Train. If it was a $1000 contest, I won it, $500 contest, my money. It was crazy man! One $1000 contest event went absolutely haywire!

Griff decided to give away a $1000 grand prize and everyone knew that I was going to win it, hands down! There really wasn't a need to go through the motions of having a lineup, when ultimately, the crowd would persuade the judges to give the money to MISTER.

On the Sunday before that Wednesday, I had sprained my ankle badly, playing ball in College Park. I really didn't think I would be able to perform at all. I couldn't stand or walk on my foot. I iced it over and over for the next three days, trying to at least be able to stand up without falling. I was also practicing my show routine for the contest. I was going to perform over the new Eminem track, "Shady's Back."

I rapped like him but changed the words to mention everybody in the Red Train and made it very relevant. It was going to be crazy! I wrapped my foot in about 3 pair of socks and slid it into an ankle-high timberland boot to keep it stiff. I donned a Cincinnati Red outfit, black-red-white all over! I had my crew with me and everything! The whole night was crazy!

Every person that went up got booed within seconds of their performance. Even people who had never been booed before, who had great performances, were getting booed. After every performance, the crowd was yelling for MISTER to get on the stage. Griff was extremely upset how everyone was acting though, and rightfully so, because the crowd was being totally unfair.

Even though, it was to my benefit, I didn't want to lose the respect of my peers that were doing their thing this whole time. Griff held me off till last and once I got up there, the crowd went stupid. I couldn't even get into the whole set, before it got out of control! People rushed the stage again, Cowboy started switching up hot track after hot track, and I went off on a freestyle binge!

Jason Terry, who played for the Atlanta Hawks, was there that night as one of the judges. He was giving away tickets to his celebrity basketball event at that time. He walked up to the stage in the middle of the ruckus to personally, hand me the tickets to his event! We eventually exchanged numbers and everything!

After my performance, in which Griff had to stop abruptly, the crowd calmed down and Griff decided, in all fairness, NOT to give me the $1000 reward. He chose to only give out $500 to somebody that was pop-locking that night and gave me the other half on that next week! I felt him on that one though...the crowd was disrespectful.

After that, I pulled out of the competitions and would only rap for the fun of it, when Griff asked me to. I was done competing in there and decided to give someone else a chance to win. It was all good, because I still had the opportunity to perform and showcase my skills to a lot of the celebrity guests who would come thru. Anybody that was somebody in the city of Atlanta or the music industry that came by the Red Train, was introduced to me.

On one night, I met a producer by the name of Focus, who was signed onto Dr. Dre's Aftermath label. He was one of the judges on a night where I battled somebody and he liked what he saw. With him, was a known singer and actor, Jason Weaver, who we all know as "young Michael" in the Jacksons movie. He also was on the TV sitcom, Smart Guy, which was very popular.

They were both very genuine, humble, and cool, which you don't get to see much in the industry. We all exchanged numbers and Focus said that he would call me to do some work once he came back in town. I'm thinking, "wow, dude works with Dr. Dre!" He even played a few of his tracks and a new record he had just produced for Petey Pablo, who was hot at the time. He also played some records with a new artist by the name of The Game, which sounded dope! After hearing those tracks, I knew I needed to be on tracks of that caliber, ASAP!

On the other hand, I'm here chopping it up with Jason Weaver, about how things are about to "change drastically my n*gga" and he was right! Focus eventually called me and we all linked up. I had moved out of the All-Around Suites off Franklin Rd now and was sleeping in the corner of the living room of my man Dre's floor, off of Cascade Rd.

It was about 5-6 dudes living in the crib, but we all grew up together, so it was cool. That roster included Jules, who had moved down from VA, and who also engineered and made beats. Sheed, also down from VA, was rhyming and my right-hand man at the time, riding out everywhere. Then there was D and Seven, who were both in the military with Dre and migrated to Atlanta as well.

Nothing but music and video games went down at that spot. Some other crazy activities were going on as well, but no need to tell those stories. We can save that for Dre's book. We had a Roland 1880 that we recorded on and was knocking out song after song after song. I would use some of my Red Train money to help buy some more studio equipment to get us more up and running there.

Pooh was still recovering from being sick and unable to record, so we held it down for him. He would eventually come around to feeling better and writing again. The competition was good and I felt that the momentum I was gaining from the battle scene was just what we needed to keep pushing. Plus, I wanted my crew out there with me to rep and take this city by storm.

The energy was great and there were some great songs that came out of all that work. It felt good, we were doing the music thing, but to be honest, most of my dudes were a few years younger than me, just getting to Atlanta, and more into "the action" than the grind, so majority of the time, I was out tackling this thing myself. What I know is, I needed to make something happen and get off this floor. I had a daughter and baby mother who was living in a roommate situation of their own at the time, so I felt a sense of urgency to make something happen.

In Picture left to right: Mad Moe, Haziq, Me, Griff, Spark Dawg, Lil Flava,
Focus (at the Train)

The Pressure

It had been a while since I had spoken to Focus, perhaps too long in my mind. I was really getting fed up with my collection job and wanted something to happen at a more rapid pace than what it actually was. Remember, I had no car of my own, no shelter of my own, and always depending on someone else to take me here and there.

It sucked to be a grown man and have to depend on others. It didn't help that my child's mother, would give me the "blues" as to what I was and was not doing for her and Genesis. She was very supportive on one hand, but on the other, she wanted results…fast, seemingly impossible results!

There was a great deal of adversity when it came to chasing this "dream", as my mother and a host of others would call it. It's not uncommon to hear, "everybody can't be a star…what's your plan B?" I always approached the situation as if there is no Plan B, only Plan A, which is to succeed! Of course, it sounds good…but reality bites man, it bites hard and often. Needless to say, I pushed forward, blocking out any negative thoughts of failing.

I persistently called Focus, in order to show him that I was serious and wanted to work. We eventually talked and he agreed to pick me up and take me to his studio. I was ecstatic when he finally pulled up to the spot on Cascade Rd. He had a Volvo coupe, that I pretty much considered to be a sports car. It was kind of small, in my opinion, for the likes of Focus though.

MISTER

He appeared very much in physical, as I thought him to be in stature…big! He stood over 6 ft tall easy, kind of heavy set, but had crazy swagger…like a Heavy D of some sort.

He was tatted up crazy! For some reason, I always associated real industry guys or artists, as being these weird, tatted up guys. I don't know, it's just me…I didn't have any, so I'm already thinking of breaking promises to my mother of not getting one. I can hear her now, "you did what? I told you that rap mess ain't nothing but the Devil!"

Anyhow, we peeled out and headed back to his side of town, which was Stone Mountain. After finding out how far away he lived from me, I realized how much of a ground I gained by this guy going all out of his way to accommodate me. While we rode out, we conversed, just getting to know each other a bit. Mostly, we talked about our backgrounds, family, and music interests.

One of the main things we had in common, was our love for REAL hip hop. Focus had just moved out to Atlanta from L.A., where he had lived for a majority of his life, but his origins go back to where he was raised, on the East Coast, between the Bronx, NY and Connecticut. He was also the son of Bernard Edwards, one of the founding members of the group Chic! Now that was ironic because I used to love Chic.

My aunt Karen put me onto them years ago and used to play their cassettes to death at her house. I fell in love with the music in their songs. One of my favorite songs from them was, "I Want Your Love." It had this crazy, music breakdown at the end of the song. I used to blast it from my aunt's boom box! I might have mentioned that to him, I can't recall. It depends on whether or not I felt it to be too corny to mention at the moment.

The drive was a good 30-35 minutes away, as he lived all the way down highway 78, off of West Park Plaza exit. It seemed like going to the bat cave, heading to his house. He had a nice sized home, expected of a big-time producer. He had the studio built into one of his rooms. Once I got in the studio, I was immediately hooked! I saw all types of plaques on the wall. There were personally, signed photos from the likes of Beyonce, Christina Milian, Kandi from Xscape, and so on. I even saw a large photo of Griff on the wall, the guy that made it all happen for me.

There were all kinds of keyboards and beat machines, electric guitars, and a large monitor for his computer. So, this is where all the magic happens, I thought. Focus used to have a full bar at his house too. Around this time, Hypnotiq had just been introduced to the world. I wasn't really a fan of it too much, as I was really into Hennessey at the time.

Focus was the first to introduce me to the mixture of Hypnotiq and Hennessey. When you mix the two together, it turns green. I thought it was the coolest thing, not to mention, it was extremely tasteful and would have you buzzing in no time! I immediately gave it a nickname...I called it Alien Piss! After about a month or so, it was catching on at the clubs and people started calling it Incredible Hulk. I carried the stigma that I had *been* on that...look at me, already in my Hollywood zone!

Now that we'd enjoyed a few drinks, it was time to get to the lab. Focus had entirely too many beats in his arsenal and every one of them I wanted.

MISTER

He would play a beat, I would go crazy off of it…he would go to the next one, I would vibe out to it. It got to the point where I couldn't make my mind up, so he decided to make a beat for me from scratch. I watched him as he played samples through one of his machines, until he finally found one. He sampled it, chopped it up, looped it…then he went over to his beat machine and started banging away with some drums. Literally, 5 minutes later, it was complete.

I couldn't believe it! This guy just made a beat from scratch and it was a complete banger! Right up my alley too. He told me not to write anything to it right then, but that he wanted me to take my time with it and just vibe. He dropped me off at the crib later that night and I immediately played it for the homies. I can't even remember if they cared about the beat or not, I was too busy wrapped up in it and zoned out to care.

I would say that it took me about 3 hours to write a song to the beat. I was nervous more than anything else, because I didn't want to disappoint Focus at all and I was trying my hardest not to fold under *The Pressure*. See most "battle" rappers have this label attached to them, that they can't write a song. I'll be the first to admit, that my songwriting ability was not up to par at all. I could write lyrics for days, but to put them into sequence and cadence to where the listener could enjoy it to the point of it being a recording "hit", was another story.

So here I was, writing diligently trying to make sure that this song impresses Focus enough to make him want to keep working with me. After I finished writing the song, I practiced it over and over, until I had it down pat. Once I knew that it was ready to record, I hit up Focus, anxiously, to let him know that I was done with the track…it was time to record it!

The recording process was like I had never done before. Once I got in the booth, I felt nervous and anxious at the same time. I hadn't memorized the rhyme completely, so I had to read it under the black light that was in the booth. I remember him telling me to relax. Relax? I'm thinking that this guy has been in studios with the likes of Destiny's Child, Dr. Dre, 50 Cent, Eminem, and so on. "Relax" was the furthest thing from my mind, I felt a huge amount of pressure to show that I had something just as special.

He had me get something to drink, so I grabbed a glass of Alien Piss and let him know that I needed to smoke real quick. Focus didn't smoke at all, but I frequently indulged with Mary Jane. The smoking area was the garage, so I went there to smoke and ease some of the pressure off of me. It didn't take long before I was relaxed enough to hit the booth again. Once I heard the loud music in the headphones beating and my voice amplified over it, it was officially on!

I spit my verses with conviction and Focus just let me go. The only thing he did, was have me stack the hook like 8 times! I didn't understand why I had to stack a hook 8 times back then, but now I understand that it gives the chorus effect and makes the vocals standout from the verse. From Focus, I learned the basics of how far back to stand from the mic, which words to emphasize on the stacks, and how "less is more."

Before, I used to stack my verses word for word and have crazy adlibs in the background. I realized that it didn't take all of that to make a good song. I had finally finished laying the whole song, and it was time to listen. Focus didn't take long putting a quick mix on it, though his mix sounded like a professional mix and mastered version. It was a complete upgrade from the quality of my previous work.

He played the song back, over and over, tweaking it a little bit at a time, until it was finally to his satisfaction. It was already to my satisfaction, once I heard it played back the first time. He lifted my whole spirits when he told me that it was a hot record! What?!! Yes, I had done it! This meant more work, it had to!

He said that we would keep doing more records, so he gave me a cd of some more beats that he had to see what I could come up with. Cool, I took the beat cd home, along with my new song! The homies, back at the crib, was loving the song! I remembered Dre asking to ride to the store with the song. I let him, and he came back like, "that song is a banger…I had it on repeat the whole time."

It didn't stop there, we listened to the song all night on repeat. I swear that song must have played all night and put us all to sleep. I felt so proud of this one little accomplishment of recording a song with a real, industry producer…Aftermath Ent. Producer, Focus!

Of course, I took the song to the Red Train on a packed Wednesday and Griff was, and is to this day one of my greatest supporters! He introduced the new record to the packed house, "this is the new record with Mr. Ripley, produced by Aftermath's own Focus…check it out!"

DJ Cowboy put the song on, and the track hit so loud and hard, that I was completely astonished at the reaction. The crowd was loving the song!

Of course, Griff would stop Cowboy, and tell him to run it back over and over again. It was if I had made it already, by the way people were coming up to me and congratulating me on the song. I recall being in the back seat of a drop top convertible at night, riding down Franklin Rd., with a couple of lady friends. The song was blasting thru the speakers, even against the wind of the night.

> **"Sure, as time is ticking, it's money out there, it's time we get it**
> **We all lust the good life, say it's time we live it,**
> **Put your glass of champagne up, wet the game up, sky's the limit".**
> - <u>Sky's The Limit</u>

MISTER

Grammy winning and Aftermath producer, Focus...

Crew

I really felt a sense of accomplishment and that I was finally on my way to getting on the Inside. I stayed on task, by writing to as many beats as possible, from the cd Focus had given to me earlier. The beats were what I would consider "warm up" beats. He was trying to test my songwriting ability, as far as, coming up with a commercial record now.

I had knocked out about 4-5 beats off of the cd and was anxious to let him hear what I had come up with. I surprised myself with the concepts and themes I had come up with. I was challenging myself to become a real songwriter. Focus met up with me, while I was visiting my daughter. When he got there, he got a chance to meet the daughter that I raved about so much.

Genesis was barely two years old and was just as loveable as she could be. Being that Focus was a single parent of 2 himself, I think he took a liking to the fact that I was a responsible father and was really trying to do right by my family. I played the beat cd he had given me and let him hear a few of the songs that I had come up with. He seemed to like the songs, one in particular, called "Street Sweeperz."

He ended up giving me another beat that he felt would go better with it, in which it did. I had one of my people, Sheed, drive me out to Focus' studio so that I could get some more work in. Sheed was one of the homies that hung around Dre, back in VA. He worked with me at the collection job and basically ended up being one of my rides everywhere.

On this trip to Focus' crib, I was going to record this Street Sweeperz song. Focus felt that the hook was hot, but needed a different voice, so he asked Sheed to spit the hook. Focus immediately took a liking to Sheed's voice and asked him to spit something, in which, Sheed did and murdered a few verses. I was proud of the homie and happy that he confirmed even more that VA had some real spitters. If he was as hungry as I was, it's my feeling that he would have taken off immediately. I know Focus felt the same way, he constantly wanted Sheed to record more music.

For some reason, I guess he didn't care much for the hustle and bustle I was dealing with. Either way, once I blew up, the whole crew was coming with me anyway, so it really didn't matter. The whole purpose was to get in the door and bring the family with you….at least that was the plan.

The records were coming along well, and you could hear the growth with each song. The great thing about Focus was that he was passionate about his craft, and really liked for the process to be organic. He had a way of recording that was very meticulous, and he challenged me a lot. In the beginning, he would just play something that catered to my style of straight forward lyrical wordplay, but he also gave a variety of production to practice different writing approaches. "For Hire" is a record that we did together, that was an example of just that.

The track required for me to be less wordy and more rhyme catchy. The hook was my best effort of a sing along, in my opinion. Nevertheless, it showed that I was capable of switching up the styles and could write a record that was completely outside of my box.

> "…they wanna know who is he, got all his n****z wit em
> straight out that Ol Virginee, my 7th day committee
> got any problems wit me, my n****z cock da semis
> we flood yo block with millis, that's word to Krook n Gimme
> ….I'm for hire, I'm for hire, I'm for hire, I'm for hire"
> - **For Hire**

After getting the song mixed how he liked it, I took it down to the Red Train and had Griff debut the record for the hundreds in attendance. It felt good to, once again, hear my voice blasting thru the club speakers and to see the entire crowd's reaction. It's a feeling I'd like to have over and over again.

Around this time, the grind was in full swing. I was in the studio almost every day, either at Focus' spot or working back at the crash spot in L3 off Cascade with the home setup we had. It was during this time that I accumulated most of my catalog of music and rhymes that I have archived to date.

If I wasn't at the studio, I was out in the streets, everywhere networking and linking up with different social circles in the industry. These were also the times when I would start to get befriended by celebrities that lived in the city. Focus worked with a lot of celebrity artists, so thru him, I had met Kandi from the R&B group, Xscape, that was signed to Jermaine Dupri at So So

MISTER

Def, also rap artist Sole, to name a couple. Focus produced for groups of his own that was a part of his label called, aFocaliptic or AFam records.

The artists were rap group, Misery Ill and Komplete, the R&B group. He, of course, was also working with Jason Weaver, who was part of the AFam. Everyone would be over at Focus spot often. All we did, was hangout and <u>make music</u>. The chemistry was immediate and I was officially a part of the *Crew*. O Grimes, of Misery Ill and I would connect from time to time and kick it. That guy was full of character.

Thru him, I met a producer and songwriter by the name of Mistah Raja, who has worked with many platinum artists in the game. He had a brother that was real cool named Reg Raw. Also, there was Isaac Hayes III, son of the music legend, Isaac Hayes, producer Sef Millz, and NBA player "Big Dog" Glenn Robinson. J Weave and I had developed what I would call an industry friendship right away, that transcended to real life.

My girl and I would hang out with him and his lady from time to time. We'd watch each other's kids and the whole nine. I figured him to be a real, genuine dude. I appreciated all the game he would give me about the entertainment field as far as what and who to look out for. He always had some jewels to give me and we would link to do music or just hang out. I mean, how incredible was it to get first hand insight on how to maneuver in the game.

J Weave was getting checks from music, TV, and film. He would always say that it "ain't no money like that Disney money." After kicking it with him so much, you almost forget that this guy was the singing voice for Simba in Lion King. The Hollywood stories I would hear from J Weave are all movies that need to be made. I used to trip out, like I really have this celebrity friend, that knows Me and hits ME up to roll out with and do work in the studio. Like…this is crazy!

I would recall that my man Derek, the twin, back at FAMU, would say that he was related to Jason Weaver. Derek was also living in the A, with his brother Erick. There crib was also one of my many stops on the floor when I was homeless. He would always try and get me to tell J Weave about him…which I would never do. I never wanted to appear or come off like an annoying groupie around celeb figures. I used to treat those relationships very delicate.

I used to think that it was hard enough just trying to make these connections in the first place, I can't afford to lose them…at least not right now. As chance would have it though, I had a get together for my birthday. I invited the twins, Erick and Derek, to hang out, along with some other of my guys. It had to be Flick, who I was still rolling tight with, and maybe his homie, Jeff was with us.

They all met up with me at my girl's spot. I got a call from J Weave and Focus, saying they were coming through to celebrate with me too. So, this would be like the first time I have my industry friends hang with my day-one friends. It wasn't until J Weave and Focus arrived, that I realized I had Jason Weaver and Derek in the same place at the same time.

You guessed it, Derek started to tell J Weave how they were cousins and they have the same relatives back home in Chicago. Long story short, after both parties are on the phone with their family back home, a direct connection was made to confirm that they were indeed related…and closely related, at that.

This family tree extended to a couple of other music industry playmakers, Kuk Harrell (Grammy award winning songwriter and producer-credited work for Rihanna, JLo, Beyonce, Chris Brown, Mary J Blige) and Tricky Stewart (Grammy award winning producer and songwriter-credited work for Justin Bieber, Rihanna, Beyonce, Britney Spears).

The descriptions don't even scratch the surface of the accomplishments and collaborations that these guys have done. Look these names up to get more details on the impact they have in the game. Your top 10 songs on radio in the last 20 years, have most likely been produced, written, or engineered by these gentlemen. My readers who are In the game definitely know most of these names. Bottom line, the Twins cousins are "kind of a big deal."

So now that we are all one big happy family, with both sides of my friends clicking, we all went out to the club and had the time of our lives. We hit up the Buckhead strip and landed at Club Shadows, the infamous club where the Ray Lewis incident happened just a few years earlier.

We walked up…No line, straight VIP, bottles, bottles, and more bottles. Hot 107.9 was hosting the party that night, in which I received numerous radio shout outs. The R&B group, Jagged Edge, was in the building partying with us as well. I was in there with my crew, my industry homies, bottles to the head, and on cloud nine.

Focus kept passing me bottles of Hypnotiq all night and it felt good to have all my peoples in one spot together having a blast. I remember J Weave, who had more fun than me on my own birthday, put his arm around my neck and said "get used to this ma n***a…you In here boy."

My dude got so wasted that we had to sneak him out the back of the club, so no paparazzi would try to catch him in that state. I certainly held him down and made sure he got home safe to the crib. We laughed and joked about it afterwards back at his place. We would go on to share a lot of good times and great talks. I learned a great deal about the entertainment business from J Weave, real genuine dude.

Kicking back with the homie, Jason Weaver aka J Weave

Picture left to right: J Weave, Dez Griffin, Me, Spark Dawg

Keep It Rollin'

You couldn't tell me that I wasn't on the right path at this point. I had linked with a super producer, had a huge fan base of supporters on the northside of Atlanta, getting my name out there in the underground scene, as well as, connecting with a wide range of mainstream heavy hitters.

I was meeting major players that did magic behind the scene and have no clue as to the weight they held in the game, treating their business cards like collectible items. In my mind, I still had a way to go and more people to meet. I had to *Keep It Rollin*…there was more work to do.

I recall connecting with a guy by the name of Shakir Stewart, who had come by the Red Train and caught my performance. He was working with a company called HITCO, which I was not too familiar with, at the time, but in hindsight, I really needed to look no further, as far as connections to "the Inside" was concerned.

There was also a producer who I met, named Shondrae, later went by the name of Bangladesh, who has a number of hits under his belt. He worked out of a spot called Patchwerk Studios, which I noticed from the credits on a couple of Outkast projects, and a few other artists.

I developed a relationship with Delino DeShields, a former MLB player, who had started a record label called 502 records, which represented the area code where he was from in Delaware. He had a couple of artists that he requested me to collab with and work out of his studio that he had on the southside of town off Fairburn Rd.

Delino was the reason I was able to record my only record with NO I.D., whom he had helping with production on his label. The track was so melodic and was typical of the NO I.D. sound. I was so thrilled at the opportunity to put down vocals on his track. The song was a collab with one of Delino's artists, called "We Peoples."

We knocked out a few records under 502 that never saw the light of day and I'm not sure of whatever became of the label. Still, I was appreciative of the opportunity. I even brought Pooh, who was coming around to feeling a little better from being sick, to the 502 studio with me to knock out a record. He was happy and it was good to have him back out in the loop.

In the end, I was able to leave with two tracks from NO I.D. on the resume, so I was happy. It's not every day you can share the same producer with the likes of Jay Z, Kanye, Common, and J Cole, to name a few.

A lot of the things going on was happening so fast, so much that most of it is a blur really. Every day was an adventure. I was literally broke, with only money that I would win from battling, sleeping on the floor, here and there. Thank God for the friends that looked out for me during this time. I was in an unstable relationship, I was going through it.

I was hustling everything from fruit, water, weed, CDs, and porn DVDs to make ends meet. Yet, I was having the time of my life along the way. I was making my waves across the town and getting my network on heavy. I remember, Griff, took me with him to attend a Falcons game. We had seats in the suite with Brian Jordan, who was a celebrity, former Falcons and

Braves player. We went to watch Mike Vick run all over Julius Peppers, and the Carolina Panthers. Drinks and food were all complimentary and it was the first time I had experienced something like this.

After the game, we were granted access to the players locker area, where we would meet with one of the starting safeties, Ray Buchanan. Fast forward, an hour or so later, we were pulling up to Ray's mansion out in Sugarloaf. By the time we arrived, Ray had just taken a couple of friends around the mansion on a tour and said he was too tired to go another round. I was buggin off that statement alone.

We made our way to the basement, which was a house in and of itself. The basement had like 3 bedrooms, full bath, bar area, and a movie theater. I remember he had this long hallway lined with life-size posters of himself against all pro wide receivers. He had everyone from Jerry Rice, Chris Carter, and even had a photo of himself lined up against Deion Sanders. The most prized possession I noticed, was an autographed football from Dan Marino. Being the huge Miami Dolphins fan that I am, I was floored. Turns out, the very first interception that Ray Buchanan had in the NFL was a ball thrown by Dan Marino. Being a fan himself, he got ole' Dan to sign it for him. Dope!

The excitement didn't stop there, as Ray had DJ Casper hanging out with us. DJ Casper was known for one of the biggest records out at the time, called the Cha Cha Slide. As I'm sitting at the bar, going in for another drink, two more guests walked in, to my surprise. It was Mike Vick! I'm like, Wow, is this real?!

MISTER

One day, I'm sleeping on the floor, trying to figure out where the next meal is coming from. The next, I'm attending a Falcons game, with a seat in the suite, to later lounging at a mansion of one of the star players, and the star player of the entire NFL league! This was all too exciting, and I was doing my best impression of keeping it cool, like all of this was normal. I introduced myself to Mike, who had his brother, Marcus, with him as well. We briefly talked about VA and kept it moving. We all would later head to the theater to watch the movie, Pearl Harbor. I couldn't wait to tell the homies about the day I had, though, I can't remember if I even did or not. These types of spontaneous moments were beginning to be a thing of the norm.

The list of connections kept growing and I was able to maneuver in the city, by being in the place to be, with a whole new social circle of high clientele. It was around this same time, that I had also linked with Jason Terry, NBA player, and starting point guard for the Atlanta Hawks.

We first met back when he was a celebrity guest judge at the Gong show at Café Red Train. In the middle of my performance that night, he came to the front of the stage and handed me the winning tickets to attend his celebrity basketball game. He also gave me his personal cell phone number to stay in touch. I soon reached out to him to ask him for some extra tickets to bring a few of my homies with me to the game. He had me meet up with him at Marietta Lanes out on my side of town on the Northside.

We chopped it up for a second and he told me that after the game, he wanted me to link up with him at the studio to do some work with the Outlaws. Wait a minute…huh? The Outlaws?? This group was a part of the biggest movements and figures in Hip Hop, Tupac Shakur, and Deathrow Records! Hell yeah I can meet you at the studio!

I couldn't wait for the big celebrity game day. I ended up bringing Pooh, who was still getting around to feeling better, his pops, Wendell, and I think Dre and Sheed tagged along. It was star-studded. We met and took pictures with some of the top NBA players in the league.

I was glad that I was able to have my people experience this event with me, especially Pooh, because I know he wanted to be right there beside me mashing out and making these moves. He definitely would have if he could have. It was good for him to see it and have some inspiration, knowing things are still moving. He even took a picture with professional boxers, Vernon Forrest and Roy Jones, Jr. I was excited to meet Roy Jones myself. I had previously connected with professional boxing champion, Vernon Forrest, who had just beat Sugar Shane Mosley, in an upset victory for the title. He had stopped by the Red Train and saw my performance as well and wanted me to help him out with some music projects he had been working on with his Destiny Child foundation and label.

We would hang out from time to time, riding out, talking about everything from battle rapping to Don King. Vernon also had a nice mansion located in Buckhead, off Mount Paran Rd. He was very passionate and a no-nonsense type of guy. I remember riding with him in his all black, 4.6 Range Rover, bumping TI and Jeezy.

He'd talk about haters in the city and how I needed to be careful with who I had around me, because you never know people's true intentions.

MISTER

Lifting up the middle console, he showed me that he had something for any hater that decided to roll up on him. Sadly, a few years later, he would be gunned down in a robbery attempt. I attended his funeral at New Birth Missionary Baptist Church in Lithonia, Ga. A sad day, indeed. Vernon was definitely one of the real ones I've met.

Back to this celebrity game, while we were sitting in the stands, Griff, came by and chopped it up with me for a little bit. At the same time, Yukmouth (from hip hop group, the Luniz), came over and Griff introduced as, mentioning that we should work together. Yuk exchanged numbers with me and told me to link with him later that day at the studio to record with him and the Outlaws. I told him that I was supposed to meet up with JT (Jason Terry) at the same session, so that's already a plan.

Everything was happening organically. It seems that every connection was making another connection and was tied together some way down the line. We met up at Hendu studios, which was owned by another NBA player, Allan Henderson. This is the same studio where Raja and Isaac Hayes III, who I met thru O, worked out of. I was anxious to see how everyone worked in the lab.

The record was put together by JT to have the Outlaws and Yukmouth collab for a compilation album he was releasing through his own The Reason Records label. I remember the song title called "It's Nothin." Yukmouth laid his vocals and I remember them being extra hard and energetic. Yuk is a wild dude and real fun to be around.

Interesting fact, Yuk had the phone number with an Oklahoma area code. I asked him about it and he put me on to the burner cellular connect he had going. That was crazy because we had the burner cellular back when we first moved to ATL from VA, while living on Camp Creek.

Back to the studio session with the Outlaws...only Edi and Kastro showed up to the studio to feature on the song. I chopped it up with them every now and then during the session, asking for insight and watched their crazy work ethic in the studio that was clearly influenced by Pac. We also talked about their industry experiences and how they were glad to get out of LA. Mainly due to being done with the traffic and having to go everywhere with like 10 to 20 people just to hang out due to the climate of violence and wild Hollywood drama. All of this while the beats are banging out of the soundboard, with everyone simultaneously vibing.

Once I finished writing my verse, I asked Edi to check it out, so I spit it for him. The verse, was murderous! The cloth I was cut from, represented VA pain and drama, where only aggression was the approach. Even though, in real life and in my music, there are more different layers to me that side on the level of righteousness and conscienceness, I adapted very well to this approach. Not to mention, I'm an underdog and hungry! I made a name for myself in the city by going Hard! Couple that with the fact that I was doing a song with the Outlaws and Yukmouth, two artists that know and represent that thug life to the fullest...I can't come soft and weak, I gotta BODY something!

I felt very good about the verse after kicking it to Edi. He told me that he liked it and to go hard. I asked him if it was too much "gangsta and violence" in it, to which he said something that stuck with me to this day. He simply said, "it's cool…I mean, Get It how YOU live."

That said a mouthful. Here I am trying to impress these guys with these murderous bars, knowing that they have been around and rapped with some of the most top-of-the- line gangster rappers and livest street dudes alive. There is nothing that I can spit that's going to make them believe that I'm the hardest guy out. It was silly. In the end, I didn't make the record. I don't think it was because of my verse, it may have been because I added no celebrity value to the record. Or they didn't know me like that, to just allow me on the song with them. It didn't matter that I was JT's man or not.

JT basically told me that he would need me to do another record for the compilation instead. I peeped the politics though and understood what it was. I needed to wait my turn and pay a little bit more dues. Paying these dues had me hanging out in every major studio in the city. I would be up at Hendu almost daily, just hanging out, and selling bags of smoke. I was everybody's favorite person in the studio when I showed up.

I even had a run in with my girl's ex in the studio at one point. It wasn't an altercation, just a conversation. I knew he was her ex, but he didn't know me. I knew him to be a budding rapper that featured on a number one charted song that ruled the airwaves at the time. I had hooked up with her around the same time they were still seeing each other, as his pictures used to still be on the mirror at her apartment, along with other clothing items. These clues, along with a chatty roommate, confirmed this.

I asked him about this guy who had claimed to be his manager. This same guy had approached me back at the Red Train recently, offering to manage me and name dropped a few of his clients, including this particular artist. I took it as a moment to get confirmation on the status of this guy. He downplayed the guy big time and said that's just some dude that be hanging around with him and doesn't manage him at all. He then laughed about it and we moved on.

Off that conversation, it was no surprise that I didn't follow up with the guy to give him a chance to manage me. In hindsight, this proved to be another bad judgment call, as this manager ended up being a top executive at one of the most esteemed labels in the industry at Def Jam. Ironically, our paths would cross again a couple of years later.

As for the charting rapper/girl's ex, his fifteen minutes of fame went faster than a blink of the eye, which is no shot to him at all. This business is very hard to get in, but even harder to stay in as I learned quickly. Hendu studios would be a favorite, hangout spot of mine for quite some time. I loved the atmosphere, and the environment was very inspiring.

The producers there all had that heat and would be working 24/7. Another familiar face around the studio would be the homie, Lil Jamal aka Mally G, who I always seem to run into. This guy is always "in the place to be." We would run thru bags of orange kush at the lab, rhyming.

One of the most epic nights at the studio, would be when Kurupt from the Dogg Pound showed up at Hendu. He came in with an all-black, fur coat, shades on at night, looking like a straight gangsta rap star. I was too excited (on the inside) about meeting a true legend in the game from one of the most arguably, top record labels and movements of all time, Deathrow Records. I mean, c'mon on now, the history!

On top of that, Kurupt is respected by mainstream and underground rap artists alike, for his ability to body the mic! He is one of the best freestylers in the history of the art. At this particular time, that's all I was known for and wanted to be the best at it. So, what do you think happens? You guessed it…an impromptu freestyle session for multiple rounds.

I specifically recall it being in the studio hallway. Artists were Kurupt, Lil Jamal, Reg Raw, and me. Being in that circle, added more fuel and confirmation that THIS is where I belong, I'm right at home. It felt good that I was able to hold my own against some credible artists who have been proven in the rap game. This confidence led me to taking a trip all the way to NYC for a rap battle for MTV!

My first photoshoot

Phony Rappers

I was at the studio with Focus, when the advertisement came across the TV. I was amped about it and Focus asked if I was serious about going, and if so, he'd pay my way up there. Dope! By this time, I had recorded a lot of songs, enough for a full project. I decided that I would make a trip out of it and drive to New York. That way, I could stop back home in Virginia to visit family and friends, plus hang out with my family in New York.

I didn't officially have an album to release, so I went over to Al's house to have him help me with putting together a cd of my recordings. We ended up making a full track list, designed a cover, with full credits and everything! We manually pressed up about 50 CDs, one by one, on his computer and printer.

It felt good to see my first project in that cd jacket. It had a picture of me on the front, rocking a yellow sweatsuit and an Atlanta Hawks jersey, from a photoshoot we did by Krogg Street, downtown Atlanta. The outfit was from Larry, of course. The cover also had a picture of my daughter, Genesis Lyric, on the back with the track listing.

I ended up taking those same CDs to work with me at Nationwide Credit, selling them for $10 a piece and quickly sold out! I went back to Al's to press up about 50 more, which I sold out once I took them to the Red Train. At this point, I had to find someone that could duplicate CDs in mass, so I linked up with my guy, Rodney at WHTV, who ended up getting about

200 of them pressed up for me. I then took those copies with me on my road trip to NY for the MC battle.

Along the way, I stopped and sold some CDs back in Virginia, got pulled over for speeding in Baltimore, then arrived in Brooklyn about 4am. I parked the rental car at my cousin's house, who lived off Clifton and Lafayette in Clinton Hills. Then about 6am, I caught the G train to Manhattan. When I got there, it was already a line wrapped around the block on 42nd St and Times Square. The scene was totally chaotic, as the crowd grew and the time for the event got closer.

I put my "Larry" skills to work by talking one of the security guards into letting me squeeze by the barricade to get closer to the front of the line. I'm not sure what exactly started it, but pushing and shoving started happening outside the venue, which led to a fight, that led to a crowd of people stampeding the building. A mini riot had broken out now and the cops showed up with batons on horses, to disperse the crowd. Needless to say, the event for that day was cancelled.

This is just great! I done drove hundreds of miles here for a battle that's no longer happening. So, now, there's hundreds of emcees that have traveled from around the country, in the middle of Times Square, with nothing else to do, but RHYME! About every 10 steps, there was a huddle of people, Black, White, Asian, Latino, male and female going for theirs, battling each other in the streets. It was the most bars I've heard in one place at one time and I loved every minute.

MISTER

You know I had to get mine off, with about every verse reppin VA and 7th Day, murderous bars! For the most part, there was a good number of artists that were dope, but there was also a bunch of gimmicky, *Phony Rappers* as well. It was still a pretty cool experience, nevertheless.

Since I was in New York, I went ahead and made a vacation out of it and stayed for about a week. Ironically, my old flame from Queens, who I linked up with in NY for the first time back in the day, was no longer living in the city. She had finally made it out like she wished and was living in Virginia, of all places. Wow, the irony. I had wished she was still there, as I would have loved to show her how much progress I had made so far.

I had my cousins help me sell my CDs. I found out quick that I wasn't going to sell much out here. I would run into a lot of artists who were selling their music for $3! I was laughed out of a few barber shops once I said how much I was selling my CD for. Seriously, I bounced to almost every hood in the city, to not only sell my music and touch the people, but it was also a Hip Hop tour for me, to soak up some history and see most of the landmarks that some of the greatest rap artists have put on the map.

The first spot I went to, was the easiest, because it was right down the block from my aunt's house. We walked over to Fulton and St. James place to see the house where the Notorious B.I.G. was raised. From there, my other cousin lived right off Marcy and Hart St., so I went to Marcy projects as well. I went to Throgs Neck, Southern Blvd, and Grand Concourse in the Bronx.

My cousin, Abe, lived deep off in Brownsville around Sutter and Rutland, where they were very reluctant, but went with me to cruise quietly thru Prospect, home of the rap group, MOP. It was there where we were hopped out on by undercover officers. They harassed and gave us a hard time, me especially, because of my rental car.

Oh yea, I failed to mention that my rental car was a candy apple red Chevy Camaro, with Florida plates. I stood out like no other in Brooklyn. So, after getting pulled over for a second time by undercovers right as I parked back at my aunt's house, I figured enough was enough, I was using the train.

The last cops that pulled me over was cool and let me off the hook. They saw I had a case of CDs in the trunk, and I explained that I was just there visiting for the MTV battle. There was no way I was up there to do any drug transactions, even though I had an ounce of weed below the driver's seat. They were looking for something bigger anyway. The CDs kind of helped my story a great deal. That, and the fact that my mother's prayers are unceasing.

One interesting day, I took my CDs with me to Jamaica Ave out in Queens to sell. I had to chase down a guy who snatched a CD out of my hand and took off. He had the nerve to act like I was about to assault him after he took My sh*t. He thought I was giving it to him, like mostly everybody else was doing up there, so I could hardly blame him for his reaction. I honestly ended up giving away most of my music up there.

I ran into a guy at the Coliseum Mall, who went by the name of DJ Cal Cutta. He said that he had a show that he produced on TV in Brooklyn called the BeatKap. He invited me out to his studio to spit a verse for the show.

MISTER

The irony is that he lived on the next block over from where I was staying off Clifton. I literally walked over to his studio to record my verse. That was a great experience, as well, to be way out in NY, performing on a local show for Brooklyn.

The validation from a New York DJ is also not a bad thing. It just added more and more to my confidence of pursuing this music. By the end of my stay, we would eventually ride all around the city, bumping my CD, bending every corner. One night, I got lost while driving, looked around and noticed that I was on a street called Vernon. Wasn't long before I saw the signs that said Queensbridge Housing. Anybody who knows me, can pretty much guess where my emotions were at this point. To me, personally, this was hip hop heaven! It was about 2 am so I didn't hang around there at all, just slowly drove on by, with thoughts of Mobb Deep music playing in my head, feeling both hype and warned.

That particular trip to NY is one I will never forget. The battle was postponed to a later date, which I didn't return for, but at least it allowed me the opportunity to grind it out on the road, dolo! I returned back to the ATL with a whole new level of determination and the Red Train would be the platform.

At this point I had been all over the city battling people at various venues, including the Royal Peacock, Club Masquerade, and the Apache, to name a few, but the Red Train was home to me and the one with the most notoriety, as Griff advertised the Gong Show constantly on the radio. With every announcement, he would mention my name as the reigning champ, it felt so good!

Griff later gave me an opportunity to make a jingle for the morning show he hosted for Frank Ski, which was huge! I hooked up with my homie, Mad Moe, to produce and record the song for me. It was important to me to try and pull as many of my people in with me as possible. To be able to do so, was dope. There was still much more work to be done though. I wasn't all the way Inside *yet*.

MISTER

MTV'S MC BATTLE POSTPONED

MTV, DEF JAM PLEDGE TO RESCHEDULE MC BATTLES IN NEAR FUTURE.

ARCHIVE-ROB-MANCINI
02/24/2003

Responding to requests from the New York City Police Department, MTV announced on Monday that it had postponed an MC battle scheduled to take place at the cable outlet's Times Square studios that day.

The product of a partnership between MTV and Def Jam Records, the contest was to award one aspiring rapper with $25,000 and a Def Jam recording contract. The contest was open only to the first 1000 entrants, but thousands began lining up outside MTV's Times Square studios in the wee hours of Monday morning (February 24). By Monday's morning rush, police asked that the event be canceled due to overcrowding.

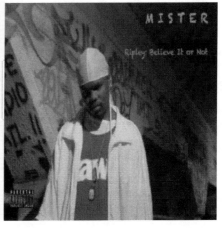

News article about MTV Battle.   Front cover of my Afam project

CD Artwork for Afam project that I sold in the streets.

God Lives Through

I had done a great job of establishing a fanbase in the North Atlanta area, mainly in Marietta, where Café Red Train was the foundation. One night, my man LA, who worked with So So Def, was in the building. He was in the VIP area on the stage and had So So Def's platinum artist, Da Brat, with him. I hadn't had a chance to run into her at all since that time at the Outkast video shoot. LA told me that he wanted to introduce us. He did, with she and I chatting for a quick second.

She saw me perform earlier and said that she thought I was dope. I gave her my number, with hopes that she would contact me soon. She was also there with Alpha T, who was a big club promoter in the city and often worked with Da Brat as her security. After hanging around for a little bit longer, they eventually left, and I told LA "good looking out" on the introduction. Hopefully, this would turn into something good.

Night after night, I was performing and battling everywhere, working harder and harder to get noticed. In the meantime, Focus was still working hard on building his own imprint with Afocaliptic Records, so I knew for certain that I would be good once his label took off.

He would often be back and forth from Los Angeles, working with Dr. Dre on his Detox project, so I would see him less and less to make music. The struggle was still very much real, because I was still crashing at different people's cribs, sleeping on couches, floors, and extended stays. The relationship with my daughter's mother was at a constant strain, because I was only passionate about "getting on" and less focused on quality time. I always said that I was out here hustling to make a better life for Genesis and her, if she stayed down. Of course, that would fall on deaf ears and add to the strife I already had outside.

The drama did make for great music in the end. Every now and then, my parents would stop in Atlanta to visit and I would let them know how I was gaining more ground with my 'devil music'. I always sought the approval of my parents on my pursuit towards this goal that they called a dream. On one visit to Atlanta, I was able to get just that.

I'm not sure what made my mom and dad want to step outside to see me perform after all of these years of me begging for their blessings on this. Whatever the reason, I was ecstatic about it! The setting, of course, was none other than the Red Train. This night was Huge!

Professional boxer, Vernon Forrest, who had literally just won the championship belt by beating undefeated boxer, Sugar Shane Mosely in an upset, was in attendance. I can't recall who else was there, but it was packed to the door, with a few great comedians as well. Zooman, Tyler, and Henry Welch were in attendance.

I gave Griff a heads up that my parents were here as well. I was very specific in explaining to Griff that this was a big deal for me. My parents were hardcore Christians, with my dad being a pastor of the church and mom, the first lady. I asked that he would *please* refrain from the normal vulgarity of his stand up and hosting. He said something to the effect of "oh ok, I got you." Cool!

I sat my parents down with me at a table that was kind of smack dab in the middle of the venue. As we're sitting there, Da Brat comes in with a small entourage and sits right next to our table. The place is going crazy, because Da Brat is always a pleasant surprise to see. She then, takes out a blunt and lights up immediately. I'm like, "damn", this is not good at all. My parents are about to run out of here and not see me perform a damn thing.

Almost on cue, Griff grabs the mic and welcomes all of the guests to the Gong Show and announces everyone in attendance. He also went on to say, and I'm paraphrasing:

> "Ladies and Gentleman we have some special guests with us tonight.
> Mister's parents are here visiting. His dad is a pastor, and his mom is the
> first lady of the church. Now, he asked me to be respectful and keep it clean
> for them....but f**k that, this is the muthaf****n Red Train and we gon
> keep this s**t all the way real, blah blah blah"

My heart was literally in my stomach, while it was turning. It felt as if a huge spotlight was over our table and I could not bring myself to make eye contact with neither my mom nor dad. Talk about embarrassed, upset, scared, just about every emotion wound up in one. Griff introduced comedian after comedian, who all upheld the traditional standard of having the most raw, vulgar, yet Hilarious content ever, with Griff in between acts pouring on more and more gasoline.

I was totally uncomfortable. I mean, one comedian, gave the most detailed account of "stealing the booty" from his girlfriend, down to how you sneak and pull the panties down with your mouth! Bruh! This night seemed like it would never end. The entire place is in an uproar of laughter, falling out of chairs, drinks are flowing, blunts are lit, I know my parents were high on contact alone.

I was completely on edge until I eventually looked at my parents to see that they were laughing themselves. This calmed me down a bit and made me relax just a little bit more. Griff finally called me to the stage to perform. I thanked my parents for showing up and proceeded to put on what I felt was the performance of my life. I kicked nothing but freestyle verses, with no profanity, and even included some lines with biblical references.

Before you know it, the whole place was on their feet, going crazy, but what I saw in the middle of all the people, in attendance brings tears to my eyes while I write this. Both of my parents were on their feet and cheering me on, along with the rest of the crowd.

I finished my show and said in the mic, that "if nothing else happens for me in this rap game, this moment is my biggest accomplishment." I hopped off the stage and gave my parents the tightest hugs, and it was very emotional. They were introduced to Griff and told him how much they loved him, that he was very funny, and that they had a great time.

To this day, my parents always ask about Griff and recall that night at the Red Train. I walked them back to the car after I performed, to see them off. They were headed back to the hotel, because it was late, but it was still early for me. They said that I made them believers in what I was doing and was totally surprised that all those people in the building were going crazy over me, their son.

They became instant supporters, which is all I ever wanted. I remember them calling me after they went to see the movie, 8 Mile, talking about this "Eminem fella" was doing what they saw me doing at the club, so if he can get on making millions, then certainly I have a chance. I told them it doesn't necessarily work like that, but I appreciate them believing in me.

The feeling was amazing, and it felt great to finally have the support of my parents. This "devil" music is not so bad after all. My dad even said something that was profound, in that, the type of response I was getting from the crowd had a sense of spirituality to it. These people are moved by what I'm saying and doing on that stage, which is similar to what he does as a preacher in the pulpit.

At the end of the day, it's about spreading Love and bringing Joy into the lives of the people. I totally got what he was saying and we both came to an agreement that even Hip Hop is the type of music that *God Lives Through*. Amen!

After my parents left the Red Train that night, I went back inside to catch up with Da Brat, because I still hadn't heard from her since I gave her my number. We talked for a little while longer, in a secluded area in the back of the spot. As we sat and talked, I told her that I really wanted an opportunity for her to check out my music and get in the studio. I remember her telling me that she meets people all the time, from all over the world that say the same thing. She went on to ask what makes me any different than them?

MISTER

I recall not really having an answer for that, but remained confident in proclaiming that I intended to make it regardless. I emphasized that I wanted her to be a part of my story. She gave me a look that kind of read "cute" and smirked. The look could have also meant "whateva n*gga", but nevertheless, she pulled out her phone and showed me that she still had my number, and she would reach out soon. I was shocked that she still had it saved and was very hopeful that I would really hear something back…soon.

Pictured left to right: Parents (Craig & Gloria), Me, sister (Kenya), brother (Rico)

Pastor Craig L. and Gloria Robinson (My Parents)

The Chase, Pt. II

Meanwhile, it was back to my collections job at Nationwide Credit, stuck on a dialer, begging folks to pay their debt off. The whole time, I'm thinking that I've got to get out of here. Bill aka Pushy, who was part of the production company, Low Frequencee, that worked with my group, Cissalc, down at FAMU, just so happened to get a position, working as an engineer for this record label, operating under MCA records.

They were working on some music for the artist, Archie Eversole, who was killing the airwaves with his "We Ready" record. Bill invited me down to the studio to chop it up with him for a second. He was working out of Zac Studios, located off Northside Drive in the city. When I got off work, I went down to catch up with him. This is one of the same studios that I had come to before, begging for someone to let me in, with no success.

So here we are for another episode of *The Chase, Pt. II*. This day, however, I had a name to drop to gain access. I was greeted by this white guy by the name of Crispy. He was super cool and showed me around the building.

The very first person I spotted was Pharrell. Never the one to be shy, I immediately yelled out his name as if we'd known each other for years, "Pharrell, what's up n*gga." He yells back, as if he'd known ME for years, like "waddup." We meet halfway in the hallway and he quickly realized that he didn't know me at all. I introduced myself, told him that I was from

Virginia too, I make music, then....out of nowhere Archie pops up speaking directly to me, super excited and was like "Yo, wassup!"

Archie then starts going on and on to Pharrell about how I was that dude, that I can spit with the best of them, about how he saw me at the Red Train, and basically gave the rest of my presentation to Pharrell himself. Talk about perfect timing, or, in this case, divine intervention. I didn't even think Archie even remembered me from the Red Train that one night, but somehow, he did.

I was shocked and feeling cocky at the same time, like "yeah, yeah, that's me." Chad, of the Neptunes, was in the cut sitting on a chair cross-legged on the drum machine. Pharrell, then said that he was busy right now working on this TLC record, but asked me to come back tomorrow, so he could put me in the booth to see how I sounded over one of his tracks. I was like, "okay!"

I chilled up there with Bill for a little longer, catching up. The fact that I had to work from 8 AM to 5 PM the next day, wasn't an afterthought, but it definitely wasn't gonna be an obstacle....I actually told my supervisor that I had a chance to work with Pharrell in the studio, so they looked out and gave no push-back on it.

It also helped that I was a top earner at the collection agency anyway. I'm pretty sure I had already met my monthly number. I always held a lot of leverage at my jobs, by overproducing, just for these types of situations here. You never know when you're gonna need to use that trump card. "Leverage" is the name of the game; the winners usually have lots of it.

MISTER

I was amped about going back to work with Pharrell the next day. I arrived at Zac studio like around 11am. Crispy greeted me again at the door. Pharrell met with me and said that he had to knock out some work first with TLC, then he'd get with me. Cool, I occupied my time by hanging out with Bill in one of the rooms, while he worked, then chilled in the lobby watching all the guests come thru.

Moment after moment, I was having watching all these artists enter the building. If you want to run into your favorite and top musicians in the game, just find your way into these studios in Atlanta. They're mostly secluded and not advertised. It's a thing you have to seek out diligently and have a way with words to gain access or a good cosign. I was in the studio right now with the best of cosigns and taking much advantage.

It was a who's who kind of day, where I was introduced to a lot of real players who operate behind the scenes. It was this day, where I met an up-and-coming producer by the name of Polow da Don. He occupied one of the smaller studio rooms and pumped out nothing but beats in there all day.

T-Boz and Chilli were both there, of course, working with Pharrell and Chad. Usher stopped by to pay Chilli a visit, as they were dating at the time. I even chilled and chopped it up with Mack 10 out in the lobby, who had his baby daughter with him. He and T-Boz were married at the time as well.

The biggest surprise came when Whitney Houston and Bobby Brown came in. I remember thinking if my brother was here, he would be losing it right now. Everyone was coming to meet with Pharrell throughout the day. Every time that he would see me, he would either acknowledge or act like I wasn't there half of the time. I didn't want to be a nuisance, so I continued to give him space until it was my time.

Hours and hours were going by, Pharrell was still busy working, had left for lunch, came back and still at it. I was trying to keep myself occupied by going from room to room, vibing with Polow one minute, then back to the lobby, then to the other room with Bill, while he was mixing, or cracking jokes with Crispy.

By now it was nightfall and I had been there since 11am, becoming a little aggravated at this point. Out of the blue, I had a phone call coming in from a private number. I answered the phone and it was Da Brat on the other end. I was extremely surprised and elated.

The call couldn't have come at a better time, because I was getting aggravated from the wait. I had to quickly remind myself that I was actually there meeting with one of the hottest producers in the game right now, while holding a conversation on the phone with one of the top music artists in the game, from the city's biggest record label. I was really feeling like I'm in a good position right now.

Brat asked me what I was up to and I told her that I was at Zac Studios waiting to meet with Pharrell. She asked how long I'd been there waiting to meet him. After hearing my answer, she asked if I was trying to keep waiting around for him, which I told her, yeah. She understood and invited me out to meet up with her after I was done. She was going to be in Buckhead at one of the clubs and said we could meet there. I told her that I would definitely see her there.

MISTER

I called my peoples and told them to meet me at the studio, because we're headed to Buckhead right after. A little while later, I'm in the booth getting entertained by one of the female groupies who was hanging around, when my peoples came in and said that Pharrell is trying to leave. I ran out of the booth to the hallway to catch the entire crew of TLC, Mack 10, Usher, Chad, and Pharrell, along with an entourage of more security and staff.

I'm pissed now that he was actually trying to leave without saying a word. I approached and his security stepped up immediately to intercede. I'm talking to Pharrell now, telling him that I'd been here all day waiting to meet with him and felt he was wrong for trying to dip out. He said that he's been busy and it got late, but then said to go ahead and let me hear what you got. This was not part of the plan at all. I reminded him that he mentioned I would be in the booth over top one of his beats. He quickly shut that down, by stating it's too late for that, either kick something for him now or he's leaving.

Now, I feel like he's carrying me in front of everybody by making me go right then, or else. So with everybody in attendance looking on, I had to just go for it. I kick the hardest verse that I could think of to start off with it and let it roll into a freestyle afterwards. I was directly in his face as if I was battle rapping against him.

When I was done, Archie, who was also there, was like "I told yall!" Pharrell gave it up to me and said that he thought I was actually dope. The bad news is that he's no longer interested in doing any rap music right now, feeling a little uninspired with it and was moving on to working with other sounds and genres. He wished me luck, turned and left. I did get pounds and nods of approval from everyone there, including major artists in the industry that night, so although I was let down, I felt a little accomplished.

On my way out, Pharrell's security came back to me and gave me a card with his cell phone number. He said that Pharrell actually liked me a lot. He just didn't want to concede in front of everyone there at the time. The security guard's name was Ben. Ben told me that Pharrell wanted me to send him my demo to the address on the card and he will consider working with me, and maybe place me on an upcoming project he had for a new artist that he signed by the name of Famlay.

Now, this was more like the response I needed. Once again, I was put in a position where I'm asked to send a demo off to an address, only this time, I was prepared. I had an entire project that I completed with Focus, I could send. All I would need to do is run it by him first. Focus recorded all of those records with me for free, with intentions of me using those records under his label, Afocaliptic. Sending the music we did to another producer, under a different umbrella doesn't make any sense at all, which is why Focus disagreed with sending him any of the records that I recorded with him.

I had nothing else to send. So, with these records being my only, quality body of work, Pharrell didn't receive the demo. But at the present moment, I was ecstatic and felt like things are headed in a great direction. My crew and I are now headed to Buckhead to meet up with Da Brat.

We get to Club Shadows before she did and grabbed a few drinks, while we were waiting. She came in with Alpha T and a few others, part of her entourage. I walked up to let her know that I was in the building and she kind of gave me the notion to come with her to the VIP section. My homies fell back and let me do my thing for the moment.

When we got to the VIP section, Brat and I sat down to chat a little bit, talking directly in each other's ear under the loud sounds of the club DJ. We smoked, drank, and I relished in the moment of being around the limelight, while everyone was stopping by, gazing at our section. After a couple of hours of that, it was time to go. I had my people come over so I could introduce them all to her. They all came over to shake hands and gave hugs prior to us leaving the club.

On the ride home, we were all hype in the car about how much fun we had inside the spot. You couldn't tell any of us nothing and that we were on the way to the top. My guy, Rock, was wilding as usual, talking about how pretty Da Brat was and that he's sure she was digging him. We all like, yeah right man, you tripping. He was adamant about it, saying when we was leaving and giving hugs, he managed to kiss her on the cheek and she didn't say nothing, like it was all good. We bust out laughing at this dude. Rock is definitely one of the bigger personalities in our crew that constantly clowned about everything, so no one was falling for that outlandish tale he was kicking. It was a fun night, and I was looking forward to a lot more.

Things were really feeling on the up and up. I was making some good ground, had a nice network going, and felt that my goal to make it on the Inside had the potential of becoming a reality. Every day was a day of grind! My work ethic was at an all-time high, but I was moving around with really no sense of direction or real plan.

I remember having feelings of anxiety a lot around this time. It was like I was standing outside a row of doors, all locked, but I'm knocking on each one, hoping one of them would let me in to see what it's like on the other side. The only tool I had was to show up and rap! No money to survive, let alone, put myself out independently. What does that look like anyway? I need a record deal and one of these doors are going to lead me to it.

A couple of them were answering the door, some were even stepping outside of the door to talk. Now, I just needed to stay consistent and persistent, and something would happen. Funny thing is, when you're moving so fast, sometimes you don't even realize how far you've actually gone. I was getting in studios that wouldn't even answer the gate at first.

A normal day for me would be riding out with Focus, vibing to beats, and recording to platinum tracks…complimentary, I might add. One of the homies, was a renowned actor and musician, who I also collaborated with on songs. I was learning to compose radio records, improving my songwriting skills, all the while studying and experiencing the politics of the game, which you can't buy. On the drop of a dime, I would be kicking it out at somebody's mansion, politicking with executives, and hanging out with celebrities like it's a thing of the norm. I could be functioning on "the Inside" and not even know it.

Part of the reason that I'm not feeling any progress, is because I'm still stuck at this collection agency in a cubicle, glued to my seat for 9 hours a day, 5 to 6 days a week. I'm still broke as hell, with little money to survive, because every dime I get is spent on extended stays, giving money to my daughter's mother, who's never satisfied, and maintaining an aspiring artist lifestyle of paying to get in open mic competitions, club access, drinks, and weed to smoke.

I had lost my car that I was sleeping out of at one point, which was the Ford wagon I received from my great-grandmother when she passed away. It was now in some impound and I had no money to get it out. This meant that I was hitching rides everywhere. My drivers/real "ridaz" were Flick, Sheed, and sometimes Dre.

Everybody, at some point, would lend their keys for me to make things happen. I also had a couple "homegirls" that held me down with a place to stay and a car to use when I needed, which I was very appreciative of. At the end of the day, given all of the drama I was having in my relationship, it was pretty nonexistent at this point, so it was cool to have some close friends hold me down.

The love was real and so was the hate, so I constantly had to keep my head on a swivel for opportunists. Usually, I would be apart from my VA homies, who lived on the Southside, SWATs area. Being that I worked and resided on the Northside of Atlanta for quite some time, I had a solid team of street homies that were playing no games when it came to me out there, especially my brother Flick and my homie Mad Moe.

Things would get crazy out in Murdaretta, which is a movie of its own. The main thing was that I needed to stay alive and focused while running thru this city, I was proclaiming to take over. I was about 150 lbs. soaking wet and a few inches "north of a dwarf", so precautionary measures were important. Having a good team around you is very important and you have to make sure that the people around you have your best interest at heart in their decision making, as I would learn soon enough.

Zac Studios

Chad and Pharrell in the studio

Archie Eversole

Club Shadows, formerly Cobalt, Buckhead, ATL

At the club with Da Brat

MISTER

Separate/Together

It had been a few months since I had heard from Da Brat. I never had her phone number, so I couldn't reach out to her, plus whenever she did call, it would be from a private line. After not hearing anything for this long of a time, I kind of chalked it up as another potential opportunity that fell to the wayside.

I recall thinking that these industry people are unpredictable, confusing, and elusive as hell. I was at the Galleria mall, having a drink with a couple of friends at a bar when I got an incoming call from a private line. It was Da Brat!

She asked what I was doing and told me that she wanted me to come to the studio later that night and gave me the address. I needed a ride, so I had Flick drive me over to the studio. While we were driving to the location of the address she gave, I'm looking around at the neighborhood and the feeling was very nostalgic. It seemed like I had been in this area before.

We, for sure, were not going to So So Def studios. This spot was closer to us out in Cobb, down Austell Rd. We got to the spot and I'm almost sure that I'd been to this place before. Once we got inside, it all came to me. The gentleman who answered the door to let us in was the same guy from years ago that we visited. It was Dion, the guy who said he knew Da Brat and that she worked out of his studio. I remember he had the dog over there and said he was babysitting the dog for Brat. Apparently, this guy was telling the truth all along.

The irony of this, that almost 4 years later, I'm back at the same spot meeting with the very same artist that we were aiming to connect with, who years prior to that, I had met at the Outkast video shoot at Freaknik. What a coincidence! Me and Dion talked about that moment of meeting him years ago, to which I acknowledged that I thought he was misleading us. Sometimes you just never know. It was just good to have something in common in the entire ordeal, as if all of this was meant to be. Brat and I proceeded to head into the studio, while Flick and Dion chilled out in the seating area.

Brat was seated at the mixing board, with an oversized Starter jacket. This was the first time that I was able to look at her and was a little surprised by her mannerisms. What I know her to be, is this brash, foul-mouthed, baggy clothes wearing, round da way girl from the hood. I expected her to be dapping me up extra hard, talking deep and acting all hard like the persona I had seen on TV. Not at all!

She was very sweet, talked softly, and carried herself very much so like that of a lady. Her nails were painted and dazzled out, hair braided nice under the cocked ball cap, and her skin looked flawless. I remember thinking to myself, like "damn, she pretty as hell." I instantly was hooked on wanting to just be around her.

The setting was real cool and laid back. There was a glass door that separated the actual studio room from the seating area, where Flick was just chilling at, waiting on me. It was at this time that Brat and I picked up on our last conversation from the Red Train, when she asked what made my story so different to where she should give me a chance.

She asked a lot of personal questions about what I had going on, job, relationship, etc.…all this, as she rolls up some weed into a Swisher Cigarillo. We went over a little bit about the politics of the music industry, discussing key points on how it's not all what it's cracked up to be. It's a shrewd business, you have to work hard, there are no promises of making it big, how loyalty is very important, and to be careful of the people you have around you.

She asked about the guys that I had with me at the club the night we met up in Buckhead and wanted to know if we were in a group or something. Her main reason for asking was because she had concerns on whether or not they would have a problem if I was to do my own thing solo, without them. I assured her that it would be no problem and they would support me regardless. Plus, I would be bringing them along with me once I got things popping.

She asked me if I trusted them like that and I told her, yeah. She then goes on to say that my crew was one of the main reasons that had her questioning whether to rock with me or not, bringing up the incident of one of the people with me who took it upon themselves to lick her neck when she gave them a hug.

I immediately flashed back to the conversation in the car with Rock telling us that he kissed her. I can't believe it, this dude was telling the truth, he actually did it! Brat said that she was so pissed about it and wanted to go off on him but didn't want to cause a scene with it being my peoples.

Her logic was if these are the type of people you hang with, then what type of person am I? Can I be trusted? Am I just as reckless? That one act could have ruined my entire opportunity. She mentioned that I should be more careful about who I bring around to certain things, because your circle could mess things up for you. I strongly took note of that and told her that something like that would never happen again. I also told her that my guy is really a solid dude that just likes to clown around at times, it wasn't no disrespect intended like that at all.

Let's just say that was a hard sell that never made it to the register. We moved on from that with her telling me that she would give me a shot, to see what I'm about. She had Dion put on some beats and she had me kick some rhymes for her over them. We vibed for a good while, with Flick even joining in with a freestyle, giving everybody a good laugh.

We had a great time at the studio. Before we left, Brat put on Kelly Price "Friend of Mine", while at the boards and sang along to every note and with every emotion. After that, we left. Leaving that studio, something was in the air. I was feeling it. This is really happening, I thought. I had to make this work! I made the conscience decision right then and there to narrow my circle and take every opportunity more seriously.

I was beginning to learn that the music game has a totally different set of codes that can easily break an opportunity for someone if violated. I had to switch things up a bit on how I moved. The plan was always to bring my team along, just like any of them would if in the same position. We were doing this, not *Separate, but Together.* I just needed to cement my position in there first, so it was time to play the game.

MISTER – POOH – DRE – MIKE – RALPH – LARRY (Just a few of my Day Ones)

Glamour and Glitz

After that studio session, Brat invited me out again to Dion's spot to vibe out a couple more times. This led to her finally giving me her phone number, so no more private number calls. I felt like a graduated and turned my tassel to the left, I guess, because I don't know what it's actually like to graduate.

Anyhow, I remember signing the project that I did and gave her a copy to have for herself. I was very proud of it and it showed. That's when she took notice of my daughter, Genesis, who was on the back cover. She thought it was dope that I had her picture on there. I honestly didn't expect her to actually listen to it, but she did.

She called me up one day and asked me to meet her up at Southside Studio, which is the official name of So So Def's recording studio. She told me to have a verse ready to kick, in case JD was there, and that I should kick that verse from the WDND song I had on my cd. This was proof that she actually listened to it. She said I snapped on that one, as opposed to any of the others and I agreed.

I'll never forget my first time walking in Southside Studios. First, the building was in the cut off I-85, north of the city. You would never know that it was there, unless you knew that it was there. The outside of the building is totally unassuming, except for a couple of nice cars parked outside. Once you make it in and thru the next two doors that you have to get buzzed through, you enter the infamous hallway lined with nothing but gold and platinum plaques on both sides.

All of So So Def's artists are on the wall, along with other top artists such as Monica, Ludacris, Usher, and Mariah Carey to name a few, and I am naming a few! The hallway leads to an open bar area and kitchen space. On the backside of this kitchen space is the boom-boom room, where there is a full stage with a convenient stripper pole in the corner, with another full bar and studio to record. This room is my favorite by far. Around the corner from there, are the restrooms, with full showers and locker rooms that lead out to a full gymnasium with a basketball court. The Afroman logo sits at the center of the court, with workout equipment in the back corner of the gymnasium.

This is where Brat and I were chilling, just talking, when Jermaine Dupri walked in. I did my best to act normal, as Brat introduced us. On the inside, I was prepping my hot 16 to drop at any given moment. After some small talk, he said that he was headed to the main studio to work on some beats.

We followed him out the gymnasium, passed thru the game room, which housed a couple of JD's pet parrots, that led out to the open kitchen area. Just left, before heading back down the hallway to exit the building, was an entrance to the main studio. This studio was huge, with a nice size room connected to it, which was the booth.

Looking around the main studio, I noticed that JD and I had similar interests, as the studio was loaded with Star Wars regalia, from R2D2, Darth Vader, and more. Also, along all of the doors and walls was nothing but pictures from magazines of just about every beautiful woman in the world, celebrities included, in bikinis. This had to be for inspiration while working. I was totally digging the environment.

At this time, Brat was in the middle of finishing up an album that was to be released soon. She was just coming off the platinum success of her last album, Unrestricted, that boasted the hit single with Tyrese, called "What Do You Like" and the other banger, "That's What I'm Looking Fo". The anticipation was high and all the energy in the studio was aimed at delivering another solid follow-up.

JD played a few beats for Brat to pick from, to which she began working on. I was amazed to be able to witness the two of them at work. So, this is what it looks like on the Inside, I'm thinking. The whole time, I'm looking at these two and playing back the history in my head....the hit records, Kris Kross, "in my bed remix", the B side, 95 Source Awards performance, so on and so on.

I couldn't believe that I was actually in the lab with them, let alone being able to participate. Brat told me to write something to the beat as well. She told me it ain't no guarantee that you'll make the record, but you should write to every one of them anyway, just in case. If not for nothing, you can brush up on your songwriting skills. She was right, I pulled out my rhyme journal and got busy.

To describe Jermaine Dupri, the Grammy award winning producer and music mogul, I would say that he is a machine! He literally lives in the studio and in conversation, you quickly learn that his musical IQ is extraordinary. First off, he doesn't talk much to begin with. After Brat introduced us that first day, even though I was around, he wouldn't say more than two words to me, if that. His head was either stuck in the beat machine, in his phone, or the video games, which he played often.

I certainly didn't take him being non conversational, personal at all. I was the new kid on the block. I was aware that Brat had an artist before named 22. I wasn't exactly sure on what happened with him, but I felt that JD wasn't too much interested in seeing anybody new come around, trying to get down. All the focus was on his franchise artist, in Da Brat and whoever she had hanging around her, that's her business.

That's the vibe I got from JD, in the beginning. I was happy to just be in the presence of greatness, so I was fine at keeping my mouth shut, speaking when spoken to, and writing. I didn't want to do anything to ruin any opportunities. So every time I came to the studio, I was in humble, work mode!

JD didn't allow for anyone to smoke in his studio, so whenever Brat and I would have to take a smoke break, we would go to the locker room or in the garage. In both of these places is usually where the freestyle session would pop off. What I would soon find out, is that Brat was a great freestyler and was actually known in the industry as such…. a pure artist.

We would go round and round with the rhymes. I think with every freestyle session, she would gain more and more confidence in her decision to rock with me and give me a shot. She was working hard on promoting and gearing up for the release of her new project and with that, she was

MISTER

scheduled to shoot a music video for her lead single, called "I'm in Luv Wit U".

The record was produced by a longtime friend of hers, LT Hutton, and featured a new R&B group by the name of Cherish. The video shoot was going to be shot down in Miami. I remember telling her that I would love to go. I'll never forget the day. I was at work, when she hit my phone. I ran to the break room to talk. She asked if I seriously wanted to come to the video shoot and if so, she would get me a plane ticket to fly down. What?! Hell yeah I wanted to go!

I had my bags packed quicker than you can say South Beach. The entire experience of this video shoot was remarkable from the jump. First of all, once I got to the airport, I had my ticket printed out and found out that I had First Class seats! I had never flown first class before in my life. So you can imagine how I felt responding to the flight attendant about what type of alcoholic beverage I would like. I am absolutely loving the reclined leather seats, pillow, and blanket already!

Once I landed in Miami, I was headed down to baggage claim. While coming down the escalator, I see a sharp dressed man in a suit, holding a rectangular card up that read "Mister Overstreet." I'm like, "is this guy waiting for me?" I went up to him and asked the same question aloud to make sure I wasn't going crazy. He replied affirmative and grabbed the bag out of my hand, escorting me to my LIMO, that was waiting just outside.

Oh yea, the limo had drinks in the back that I helped myself to as well. As the air conditioner is blowing at a very comfortable rate, I'm gazing out of the window at the sunny skies and palm trees that we were passing by. It felt like I had 'made it' already. Again, is this what it feels like on the Inside?

Before long, we arrived at the Royal Palm, located on Collins. The driver passed my bag along to the bell hop, who said that he would take care of it. In the lobby of the hotel, I was greeted by and introduced to Lucy "Juice" Raoof, who was Brat's manager, along with her husband Mr. Raoof aka "Po Baby". Right there in the lobby is where I was also introduced to Brat's aunt, Gail James, who goes by "Ainey" and Brat's grandmother, who we called "Gran". Then there was Shantel aka "Tizzle". She was Brat's hair stylist from New York. Tizzle is so down to earth, fun, and so NY. She was dope with the braids. This wasn't the entourage that I was expecting at all. This was a family affair!

I immediately felt instantly welcomed and at ease. There was a lot of staff there as well, from wardrobe stylists, hair stylists, and makeup all present. It's here in the lobby that I also met the producer of the single, LT Hutton. Standing beside him, was a very peculiar gentleman by the name of Dwen. Dwen is what you would call a "queen" and was very confident, comfortable in his own skin. I have to admit, I was absolutely not used to hanging around people as such, so it took some getting used to being around Dwen.

He was a character, nonetheless, and ended up fun to be around. Another person of note, that I was introduced to, was Stephanie Gayle, who was a longtime friend of Brat's and assisted her a great deal on many things. Steph was a sweetheart out the gate, but also very much about her business.

MISTER

Between her, Juice, and Ainey, they made sure everything ran smoothly and none of them played at all.

Once everyone was situated, we headed to our rooms. I got to my room and noticed that my bag was in there already. Talk about customer service! I could really get used to this! By this time, I had met Uncle Mike, which was Brat's uncle from Chicago. Mike was her uncle, but was close in age to Brat, so they were more like brother and sister like.

Uncle Mike went everywhere with Brat, working as her assistant and performed with her onstage all over the world. Dude was super cool and we hit it off quick. The first thing he did was get me to walk with him down the strip to go get "B" something from the store. It was then, that I got rid of "Brat" and started referring to her as "B" instead.

South Beach is an amusement park for grown-ups. I can't tell you how many foreign cars and beautiful women I spotted while strolling to the store with Uncle Mike. We were about to cross the street to head over to the store, when someone yelled out for Uncle Mike. We both turned to see who it was and I almost lost it. Riding in a shiny, turquoise colored, Benz jeep, was none other than the "baddest bitch", Trina! Now, out of all the people one would hope to meet when coming to Miami, here is one of the top persons on my list and there she was!

They chopped it up real quick and he told her that we would be shooting the video later. She said that she would try and stop by. Already, I'm like this is about to be the best trip ever! Once we made it back to the hotel, we went straight to B's suite. She asked about my flight and checked to make sure I had met everybody and was good.

While there in the room, she was trying on different fits for a photo shoot that she would be doing for Smooth magazine. Surprisingly, she put on my cd that I had given her and had it playing on the low while everyone was chilling in the room. A few people asked who it was and B told them that it was me and that she was thinking about working with me as an artist.

I totally had the support of the room, with each of them reiterating that Brat doesn't just work with anybody, so if you're around, it says a lot. I appreciated all the positive input, validation, and encouragement. Now it was time to kick back and watch the pros at work. The atmosphere at South Beach was crazy, with so much going on and so many places to hit up. I don't think I got any sleep the entire time.

The actual video shoot, was an event altogether! The director was a guy by the name of Bryan Barber. He was very lively and came off like a rock star himself, totally changing my perspective on what a typical music video director looks like. The guy had so much energy and was heavily involved in every detail of the shoot, from the lighting, to the movements and direction of the other talent involved.

I was amazed at watching him work and thought that he had one of the best jobs in the world. Similar to F. Gary Gray, who I had met years ago at Freaknik for the Outkast video shoot, I actually had no idea who Bryan Barber was at the time, being that I wasn't in the industry and unaware that there are key players Inside that create the magic we see on the screen and hear on the record. Bryan would prove to be very instrumental in a lot of artists' careers, including Outkast. He directed their film debut in the movie, Idlewild. Needless to say, he has a very impressive resume.

I occupied a seat behind his director's chair, alongside Gran, and watched the monitors as they worked. There was so much fancy equipment and staff, that it felt like we were filming a movie. Being that it was shot outside on the streets and on the beach, there were plenty of onlookers that would stop and gaze at the video action. In attendance, was everyone that was there to work, and opportunists lingering around to pass out business cards and demos.

It was super dope to see Brat in her element, while performing during the shoot. She was such a natural with it and was just an all-around Superstar! In between takes, people would hound her for photos and autographs. There was no shortage of beautiful girls around for the shoot, so Uncle Mike and I had a field day with entertaining most of them, by being buffers. Just having fun, nothing crazy…at all. It felt good to know that I was a part of the crew, rather than looking for a shot.

Brat made sure to include her team in the video, so she had us sit in a separate section by ourselves, during one of the takes, and had the camera get some good shots of us. After the shoot was over, we hung out in Miami for an extra day or so to take in the nightlife. We frequented a few spots on the South Beach strip, but also ventured out to the strip club, Rolex, in Miami. If you ever been to club Rolex, then you know the kind of night we had there. If not, read up about it…I am not getting into it with this book.

One spot I will elaborate on, is Club Bed, which was back on the beach side. This club is exactly how it sounds, it was loaded with king sized and oval shaped beds all over the club. The line outside was insane, but of course, we walked right in and was escorted to our VIP section, which was a combination of beds and sheer curtains. Imagine, just standing around and seeing nothing but a sea of people, some standing, some sitting, and some doing whatever on these beds.

I posted up in the VIP section and followed suit with what everyone else was doing. We were deep in there and next to our section, was Jermaine Dupri, who had brought Janet Jackson with him to the club. This is too surreal, I was in the moment…bottles were popping, music bumping, DJ is shouting out "JD, Janet, Da Brat, So So Def in da building" and I'm there with them. Being that the scent was in the air, I rolled up a blunt and started smoking, taking it all in, enjoying myself.

All of a sudden, I felt my arm getting yanked by security. He shouted I shouldn't be smoking in the club and quickly dragged my reluctant self out the back door of the club into an alley way. I was trying to tell him the entire time that I was with So So Def, but he wasn't trying to hear it. After screaming back and forth with this guy in the alley way, LT Hutton comes out of the door to check on me, telling the security he tripping and that I was with them.

Before you know it, Brat, Uncle Mike, and a few others were all out there grabbing me and telling the security to back the hell off. The security guard got cussed out in so many urban languages. It was hilarious. I couldn't believe that they all ran to my defense like that and made sure I was good. We went back inside, where I was handed another blunt and continued to smoke. I immediately felt both empowered and entitled. That was my first official hit off "the drug" and it was good. I wanted more.

So So Def Recordings billboard

Jermaine Dupri and Da Brat

Pic of me from the "In Luv Wit U" video shoot

Show Business

Even still, at this point, it hadn't registered with me that I was somehow, actually, on the Inside. To me, the whole experience was like getting tickets to a show, with a backstage access pass. That reality hit hard once I boarded off my first-class flight back in Atlanta. The next day I was sitting back in my cubicle at Nationwide Credit. I came down off of that high extremely fast, although, just as fast, things were about to take off.

The trip to Miami was just the start. I received a call from Brat not long after. She wanted me to take a ride with her to talk. Once we linked up, we went for a ride, where she discussed a few things with me concerning everything that she has going on, with the release of the album and everything. She was saying that things were about to get very busy and asked me how serious I was about getting an opportunity.

It was a known fact that I was in a relationship, had a daughter, and a full-time job. All these things would have to be sacrificed a great deal in order to take advantage of such opportunities. She needed to know if I was good with that. Reason being, she would have to go on the road soon to tour and promote the album over the summer. She wanted me to come along as her hype man. I couldn't believe it! Now, I have a chance to go out on the road with a platinum artist and perform on stage alongside her. This was beyond a great opportunity! There was no way I could pass this up.

I told her that I definitely wanted to go and that I appreciated her for this. We were driving thru the city at this point, while she was going over some important things as it relates to how to move within this game and everything that I needed to expect in *Show Business*. Basically, if I was going to be with her all of the time, there's certain things that I can and can't do.

One of the main things was to stay on point and look out for people trying to be slick and get next to me, in order to get next to her. Don't trust anybody! Everyone is not who they claim to be. Also, anything that I do will reflect on her, with her name being in the headlines, so don't do nothing that will cause her to get in trouble. One other thing was that I would encounter a lot of celebrities, so it was very important to not act like a fan or groupie, because now "these people are your peers that are in the same business." The moment you act like you haven't seen anything or been anywhere, you separate yourself to that of an outsider and potential threat. Bottom line, "don't be acting weird."

We talked about a lot of stuff and she allowed me to drill her with question after question. The biggest question I had for her, was what it was like to work with the great, Notorious B.I.G. She just said that on top of him being the dopest rhymer ever, he was so cool, smooth as hell, super sweet, and a real good friend that she sorely missed. I only wished that I could have had the chance to work with him.

By this time, we arrived at Southside Studios. I didn't know she had to do some work, but it was cool, I loved going over there to the studio. I had my pack of cigarillos, as usual. Then she said, "you can leave that here in the car". I was confused because I always brought my weed with me to get into my zone. She said I wouldn't need it, but I could bring it if I wanted to.

MISTER

We went inside, through the infamous plaque filled hallway and ran into JD, who was in the game room. After he and Brat spoke for a quick second, we went to studio A, the main room. No one was in there at the time. We continued through the door on the opposite side that led to studio B, which was a smaller recording room, but had a bean bag seating area just outside its main area.

I was following Brat throughs the door, when she said "wassup N*gga" to a guy that was sleeping on the bean bag. He had his jacket covering his entire face, so I couldn't make out who it was, until he came from under the jacket, and I was like, "oh sh*t, Snoop!" It was none other than the Doggy Dogg himself. I quickly remembered what Brat had just said in the ride over here and maintained my excitement about meeting arguably the biggest rap star ever. No wonder I didn't need to bring my weed.

Brat introduced us and he was like, "wassup Nephew." I couldn't believe it man. He was holding a huge mason jar in his hand. I asked him what he had in the jar. He said he got it from his homie, Willie Nelson. He handed it to me to crack open and it was the most exotic smelling weed I'd ever seen. It didn't take long before we were headed to the locker room area to burn it down, remember, JD doesn't allow smoking in the studio.

About five chronic breaks later, it was to the point where I was literally hiding from Snoop to avoid having to smoke another blunt. I can't do it. I was high as I'd ever been, but trying not to be the guy who "quit" on the rotation. At the end of the day, I'm sure there are not too many who haven't quit during a session with Snoop Dogg.

After vibing out for a bit, we all left and headed to the radio station with JD. DJ and radio personality, Greg Street was live on V103, which is one of the top radio stations in the city and region for that matter. Hot 107.9 was the other. Greg Street and JD had a show on air, called So So Def radio, where JD would take over the airwaves playing whatever he wanted.

Not long after we were settled at the station, JD announces that Mobb Deep just dropped by. I'm looking around like, what?! I can't explain the levels of respect I have for these guys and their music. C'mon now, we're talking about Havoc and P! The same group that made one of the best Hip Hop records of all time with "Shook Ones." That song goes hard to this day.

Being that I'm thoroughly invested in the culture of hip hop, I certainly thought of the fact that Mobb Deep and Snoop Dogg, who were at odds back in the day during the East Coast/West Coast beef, was in the same vicinity. It would be interesting to see how they interacted with one another, but they were cool, no tension.

They brought two other artists with them as well, Nyce and 40 Glocc. It was a room full of rap artists, so it was bound to happen. JD shouted out everyone who was in the room and said we're going live. From there, it was on. 40 Glocc rhymed, Nyce rhymed, Havoc went, then P went for his….at this time, I snatched up Snoop's headphones and slid in towards the mic.

Brat was surprised and tried to stop me, but Snoop was like, "naw, he good…go and ahead get it Nephew." After P finished, I went IN! This was my moment to go for mine amongst the elite rap artists that are in the game right now. I still remember the verse I spit:

MISTER

"Yo, what these guys talkin bout mayne

Nathan fakin, rambling out they piehole, claim they caking

That's until my flockos patient, waitin

Get tired of being without dough, stickin, takin

It's breakfast on the block, early am, wakin

Cops come we scramble like eggs, from the bacon

7th day history in the making, hatin

will get you nowhere, but a-- whipped, stripped naked

birthday suit wearing a-- dude hit the pavement

sick cuz this hit here bangin, aint it

don't have to admit man, them streets gon say it

for ya, can't do nothing but sit there, take it

all up in ya face with them razors, tasers

sharp enough to shock you with them clippers, lakers

ballin a-- guys hoop with major players

pockets like books now, we major paper"

I murdered that verse! Soon as I was done, Prodigy came right back in with another one and went bananas. After that, Brat followed up, killing it as usual with her tongue-twist flow, which is hard as hell to follow. Snoop did so, righteously, with an effortless freestyle that closed it out.

I can't tell you the feeling I had just being in that room with hip hop legends, in an On-Air rhyme session for the entire region, including the city of Atlanta. You couldn't tell me that I hadn't arrived. I solidified my own self, that night, as someone who belonged in the game. I proved that I could rap with the best of them. That was such a memorable night.

The next day, we're back at the studio, but found ourselves inside a smoked-out studio A room. Mind you, this does not happen at all in JD's studio. We were just smoking out the day before in the garage and locker room area. JD was like, what can I do? It's the homie, Snoop! We chilled and watched him work on a couple of records. His cousin, Daz, who had signed with So So Def at that time, was also there. Daz is a member of the group, Dogg Pound, alongside Kurupt. This group is responsible for one of my favorite albums, Dogg Food.

Now as I think about it, I did a couple of shows with the Lady of Rage when I was in college, was in a freestyle cipher with Kurupt back at Hendu Studios and rhymed with Snoop Dogg on the airwaves. You can say that I was pretty lucky to get a chance to connect with Deathrow Records finest artists. I'll also say that, up to this point, I had been doing very well in maintaining myself and not getting 'fanned out' by the celebs I was meeting. This all changed on another day up at Southside Studios.

While chilling in studio A, Brat and I was vibing to some beats. She asked if I had some green. I was out, but told her that my man could bring me some. This was my way of trying to get my homie, Flick, to be able to come up to the studio. I just wanted him to have a chance to experience it as well. I knew that if he could bring me a bag, then it would be all good. She said it was cool, so I hit him to pull up.

MISTER

A few minutes pass and I notice someone walking their dog in the front of the studio, on the security cameras. Brat came back in and said that Janet was out front with her puppy. I'm about to lose it, knowing that The Janet Jackson is on the same premises that I'm at. I hurried and called Flick and asked how far away he was. I wanted him to pull up, like now! He was going to pull up and see Janet Jackson in the front and lose his mind. I couldn't wait for it to happen.

He said he was pulling up, but now it looked like she was on her way back inside the building. I assumed that she was going to enter back in via the garage, so I hopped up to go the opposite way towards that hallway to head outside and meet Flick. As soon as I opened the door to leave studio A, entering the hallway, I almost ran directly into "Miss Jackson", while she was walking with JD. I completely froze and had an all-out, star struck moment. "Oh my God, it's Penny!" I'm screaming inside.

I literally didn't have the words of what to say. She was so pretty and smiled at me, with the only words I could find to say, mouth wide open, gazing at her, was "hey". Still with that smile, she said hello and they kept it moving. I ran outside to see Flick and his homie, Jeff, sitting in the car. They handed me the package, but I drilled them about how they just missed Janet Jackson standing outside, walking her dog. They were so disappointed. There was also no way I could get them access inside the studio, especially with her being there. I'm barely in myself.

The good thing is, Brat wasn't around to see that star struck moment, so it went unnoticed. I did tell her all about it though. She loved to surprise me anyway, so it was all love. I think I took a week to call everybody in my family and tell them that I met Janet Jackson. This was already a roller coaster and happening so fast. My patience with the job was slim to none. It didn't help that one day, as I was sitting in the break room, the video for "In Luv Wit U" came on.

I was standing in the break room, trying to tell as many people as possible that I was in it. Towards the end of the video, there I was, with my Montreal Expos hat and Virginia throwback jersey on, making my video cameo! Seeing that video, while at work, was both bitter and sweet. It was a huge accomplishment, yet I was still there, trying to make a living. Bottom line, I wouldn't be able to make it as a star sitting in there. Also, it definitely wasn't helping my relationship.

Going out to video shoots and hanging out in the studio, rapping on air, wasn't bringing the money in to take care of my daughter, which I had to hear over and over again. To say the least, this relationship was getting tumultuous, and I was really ready to get out. The only thing keeping me in place, was my daughter. Patience, I kept telling myself. I needed to know that God was in control and that everything happens in due time. Then finally, I got the call.

MISTER

Clip taken from RAW DVD…only capture of session at V103 w/
Greg Street

Award Tour

It was now time to hit the road for this tour. The first stop was New York City! As soon as we landed, we met with Stephanie Gayle, who was managing the tour. She had the whole agenda prepared. Tizzle, who lives in NY as well, also linked with us. She would make sure our heads was hooked up and braided nice for the tour, yes, even my braids. I actually had a nice head of hair at the time.

We were doing press runs everywhere, which included stops by MTV and BET for 106 & Park, which is one of the top video shows for hip hop music. On television, the atmosphere is so energetic, filled with lots of people screaming and complete pandemonium. In person, however, it was not what I expected. I quickly found out that the show is a "production."

In between the screams and tight camera angles, are quiet on-set protocols. It was like 2 sets of bleachers that probably could seat about 30 people total. The television not only adds weight, but it also adds the illusion of mass. Anyhow, it was cool to meet AJ and Free, who were the hosts. I tried, with no luck, to enter their infamous freestyle competition, but they weren't filming that segment on this day.

Brat did a terrific job, as usual. She is so comfortable on camera and on stage. You could tell that she'd been in this business since a teen, because she moved like a veteran. You couldn't stump her, or catch her off guard in interviews, she is very quick witted. The whole time, I was taking notes, getting hands-on experience, learning professionalism and how to use your charisma to exploit your gifts. She is one of the best at it.

Between stops for the press, we went shopping for shoes and gear, cruising thru Manhattan in a stretch limo, bumping songs from Da Brat's new album, "Limelight Luv and Nightclubs." Also in rotation was, of course, Kelly Price with "Friend of Mine", Lil Mo's song, "4Ever" and the R&B group, 702's record "I Still Love You". Bonecrusher's "Neva Scared" was also in rotation. He had a remix that featured New York rappers, Camron, Jadakiss, and Busta Rhymes. The song is dangerous! We would recite Busta's verse, over and over. He killed it.

Our hotel was located right in Times Square and on the way back to it, we spotted the gigantic banner that Tower Records had of Brat, promoting her album, it was dope! After all of the running around, we needed to get settled and chill for a bit. The hotel that we were staying in was so plush. Again, the same routine of not seeing my bags from the airport to the room, was the same. I had a junior suite that boasted some of the finest in hotel linen, spacious, floor to ceiling glass windows, overlooking the city. This is the life!

Room service on demand, nice robes and slippers, with jets for the tub, seats in the shower. Since we had a little down time, Uncle Mike, stopped by the room so we could rehearse the songs that Brat performs on stage. He had me write down all of the lyrics to her songs, so that I could memorize them. It's important to know when to jump in when she takes a breath. As fun as doing shows are, everything is still very technical and has to be done right. There was a rehearsal scheduled for us while in the city as well.

It was at the rehearsal that Brat told me that she was going to give me a slot on her show, to kick a verse. I was blown away! This would allow for the entire spotlight to be on me, while I do my thing. That was very kind of her to do, because she certainly didn't have to, besides, I hadn't proven anything as far as what I could do on the big stage yet.

DJ Shakim was the man behind the wheels for us on this tour. He was very cool and shared lots of wisdom that helped me along. Shakim had been the tour DJ for Bow Wow for years and had been around the world performing for thousands of people. He emphasized to just relax; every show will get easier with time. We weren't scheduled to perform until we got to California, so during this early part of the trip, was the time to get sharp.

When it wasn't Shakim on the road with us, it was DJ Nabs, who was also signed to So So Def, but was also one of Atlanta's top on-air DJs. One of the clubs that we used to kick it at often, when we first moved to Atlanta, was Club Kaya. This club was known to be the house that Nabs built, to where he had it packed out weekly. It was DJ Nabs who was one of the first to bring Jay-Z down to perform in Atlanta, helping to grow his southern audience. He started out as the DJ for Kris Kross and had even more experience than Shakim, having toured with Michael Jackson!

Both DJ Nabs and DJ Shakim, were very instrumental in sharing their wealth of knowledge and industry experience with me, to which I was eternally grateful. Still, I really have to credit Uncle Mike for getting me, not only stage ready, but just tour ready altogether.

MISTER

We would have lots of one on ones, where he would share experiences and school me on road etiquette. You have to remember that any mistakes you make, on or off stage, falls back on B, so you can't stress enough how important it is to stay on point and focused. I made sure to do so.

B called us to her room to chill and smoke. We had just gotten some green from this connect called Cornbread, who laced us with an assortment of flavors. Not long after, Uncle Mike went to his room and I stayed in the room with B. She went into the other room of her suite to shower, while I stayed in the main living room area.

I'm watching the television, when the hotel phone rings. I answer. On the other end, someone asks to speak with "Tat Tat". I automatically assumed they were looking for B, so I said "she's unavailable right now, may I ask who's calling?" She said, "Oh, this is Mariah". My heart must have skipped a quick beat. She then asks, "who's this?". I said, "My name Mister". She said "Ohhh, Tat has told me so much about you, I can't wait to meet you later…let her know that I called". I was blushing from ear to ear and internally, losing it. "Why was that Mariah Carey on the damn phone, just now?" …asking rhetorical questions to myself.

For those that may not know, Da Brat and Mariah Carey are like best friends. It only made sense that they would link up, being that she lived in New York. B got a kick out of the story once I told her about the missed call. We definitely met up with Mariah later that evening and hung out all night.

The first stop was the studio, where she had a session, so we met up there initially. I was super quiet, extremely shy, and could not stop gazing at this superstar singer. She looked just like she does in the videos. Tall, long legs in heels. She had on the high cutoff booty shorts and button top. I remember sitting on the couch in awe. Both B and Mariah got a kick out of it when Mariah decided to sit right beside me on the couch and spark up a conversation.

I was a complete mess and held no cocky, bravado stance with her at all. I have to keep it real; I was a bit star struck for the second time. We ended up at one of Mariah's homes that she had in Manhattan. Now, just walking through her house was an *Award Tour* of its own. She occupied like the top five levels, where once you step off the elevator, you're in the home. It was almost like a dream walking around her home, seeing all of the awards, Grammys, Billboards, MTV, the list goes on.

Her closet was the size of my last apartment, like for real. I could go on and on, describing this mini palace, but the moment that stands out, was standing on her rooftop, that was accessible thru her Moroccan room. The rooftop had a view of Central Park when facing one side and a clear view of where the World Trade Center once stood prior to the events of 9/11, which now, only showed two illuminated beams that pointed skyward.

There wasn't a better time to light up and burn one, while reflecting on where I was actually standing. With it all happening so fast, I can hardly slow down enough to take it all in and notice what I've accomplished. I called my homie Flick to just share that moment with him and just express how unbelievable it was. He encouraged me to keep going and take advantage of the opportunity, expressing that it was my time, and that I earned it.

MISTER

The next day, I decided to hit up my man Ralph and update him on the latest. Surprisingly, he told me that he was actually in New York, visiting Skittles, who had moved back home to the Bronx. We made it a point for them to both come down and see me before I had to leave. It was so good to see both of them. What made it even more sweet, is that we were in another city.

I took them up to see the room, we smoked and chilled for a little bit. Before they left, I showed them the tour bus that was parked outside. They were both happy for me and it was just great energy all over. This was a long way from those Camp Creek days at the Diplomat, and yet, we were still at it. Me and Ralph would always talk about how it was "about to be on" and now look at how far we had come. It was such a great feeling.

We left New York to finish out the East/Midwest portion of the tour, but was deterred after a tragedy struck home for B. We ended up heading straight to Chicago, after our Cleveland stop, to connect with family. It was good to hangout in B's old neighborhood on the Westside of Chicago, where she got so much love. It was good to see Gran again and get some of her good cooking.

At the house, B took me to her room where she grew up at. It was cool to see that she still had posters on the wall of her favorite artists, which included a poster of Kris Kross. I'm thinking how cool that must have been for her to end up rapping alongside a group that she idolized on her wall. It brought things into perspective for me, that, everyone starts out with a dream. It's what you do to make it a reality that matters and her story is one of a kind. I can't wait for her to share it with the world.

After a few days of regrouping with the family, we took a flight from Chicago straight to Los Angeles next, where B would do more press runs, which included a stop at Paramount Studios, where they filmed Soul Train. Yes, I performed on Soul Train! The same show that we watched almost every night at my grandmother's house, with the people jam packed in a big dance room, unscrambling words on the board before commercial breaks.

I even met the great Don Cornelius, who was no longer hosting, but worked in the background. Shemar Moore was the new host, who conducted the interview with Brat on stage and we went into a lip-syncing performance in front of a crowd of about 25 or so people. Even though it was a big deal being at Soul Train, performing, I couldn't help but think that it was the biggest disappointment ever. Where was the hype, massive crowd?

Cameras were everywhere, getting every angle of the room. I promise I could touch everyone in that room in less than 60 seconds, it was that small. So, the big deal of being at Soul Train wasn't the atmosphere itself, but rather the coolness of being able to see the real production behind the scenes. It was like I had a chance to actually catch Dad putting on the Santa Claus suit or helping my parents sneak some money under my sister's pillow on behalf of the "tooth fairy."

I was really starting to see that a lot of the images and energy created on screen are 'produced'. On one hand, it's disappointing, as a fan. On the other, it's like, "look Mister, you asked to see the Inside…here it is."

The LA experience is one that needs a book of its own as well. There's something special about seeing the big LAX sign at the airport. The paparazzi are all over the place, bum-rushing you with cameras and little microphones. It seems like everyone in LA is somebody of importance, is close with someone of importance, or trying to be someone of importance. I didn't meet many normal occupation people, like someone who had a job like me, for instance, at a collection agency, in a cubicle. No, it was "I'm an actress…I'm a writer…I was a stuntman in that one movie…I model…I'm a music artist."

The stakes are high in LA and Hollywood is addicting. You can't help but be amazed by the scenery out West. The Hollywood sign can be seen in the distance, on the hills. It's nothing like being on the Hollywood walk of fame to see all of the celebrities that are forever engraved with their star. What's cooler than walking by and notice the star for Michael Jackson under your feet? I'll tell you, nothing other than meeting the legend himself…. or maybe meeting his sister, Janet.

We stayed in two different hotels, the first being on Rodeo Drive, a very popular strip of high-profile brands, that brings out A-list celebrities for shopping. The name of our hotel was called the Luxe Hotel. We then stayed at the Beverly Wilshire, which is also a very popular hotel and very expensive, I imagine. Of course, I imagine, because I noticed the receipt they slid under the door of my suite. My room was upward $500 a day for the stay.

I think it's important to remind you all that, I'm just the hype man! I'm out here moving like an artist with a hit record out, the way this travel, room and board, and shopping is setup. I'm getting car service, manicures, pedicures, and body massages at random. I was also getting per diem, which is money that you get every day for expenses, such as food. I saved that money, because I never had to pull out my wallet anywhere. I was eating a minimum of $20-$40 plates on average.

I have to say eating at all kinds of high-end restaurants was one of the highlights of the tour. LT Hutton, who produced the lead single off the album lives in LA, so he met up with us and pretty much held us down while in the city. I remember we ended up getting rid of a security guard because he was reluctant to do his job when we found ourselves at a restaurant in a gang neighborhood.

Long story short, we had LT, who was well connected and strapped for any occasion, so we were good. It was funny, because B was sporting a red bandana around her head and the security told her it wasn't a good idea for her to smoke outside. Why did he do that…it went south from there. One thing is for sure, you can't tell B what she can't do. He learned it the hard way. I kind of felt bad for him…. ahh well.

While out in LA, we also met up with Brat's sister, LisaRaye, who was a star actress and personality herself. It was a sight to see, when you're out at a public venue with two related superstars and the rest of the building is having a good time just from watching them all night. What was even better was, I was here with them and reaping all of the second hand benefits of attention. It's the whole, "you're with them, so who are you?" effect.

Constantly, both men and women alike, try relentlessly to spark conversations, yell for attention, trying to grab you, to get a second of Da Brat's time, photo, autograph, or simple, "hello". We continued to do press runs at radio stations, where B would end up freestyling on air for the city. She even pulled me in to rhyme with her at times.

The feeling of rhyming on the radio is a high of its own. That radio mic sounds like the entire world is listening. You have zero room to fumble on the rhyme or mess up by cursing. All of my ciphers and freestyle sessions that I had gone through down at FAMU, plus the open mic battling, helped me to be sharp on the radio. You must be spontaneous and quick with your thinking cap. If you mess up, only you should know that you did.

I recall one radio DJ literally crying as B freestyled for his show. She was always his favorite rapper and to have her kick legit, off-the-head, rhymes on his show did it for him. I witnessed a lot of instances of fans losing their minds over Brat. It was amazing how she was able to function when every move someone wants something from you. She couldn't afford to have a 'down day' because some fan would take it personal if she turned down a photo or autograph. Every word, every action, was being watched and judged.

I was sitting there witnessing first-hand the effects of being a celebrity. As time passed I wondered more and more if that level of celebrity was something that I even wanted. I probably would miss being able to go to the grocery store as a normal human being. Overall, she handles the whole celebrity thing very well.

In the middle of the press run, Brat and Uncle Mike, had to head back home to be with family for a couple of days. They decided it was best to leave me out in LA, to avoid flying all the way back to Atlanta, when we had a show coming up in a couple of days. They put me up in the Beverly Hotel, while they were away. I took this time to call up a few peoples that I knew out there.

I hit up Shawn "Tubby" Holiday, who was working at EMI Publishing, under a big executive by the name of "Big Jon" Platt. He and I went to school together at FAMU. I had seen him off and on over the years. He had been getting his executive grind on. We caught up for a hot sec over the phone and he mentioned that he would love to talk business with Brat about her publishing if possible. Not really knowing that side of the business, or hers for that matter, I told him that I would run it by her and see what she says. Either way, it would be good to catch up on everything he and I both had going on.

I made another call to Focus, who had relocated to LA, working on the Detox album with Dr. Dre of Aftermath Records. He came and scooped me from the hotel and we went back to Larabee North Studios to work on some music. I wrote and recorded a reference song for Dr. Dre called "Once Again." I worked on it with another artist that Focus knew, a guy named Verb. Focus was real cool with Omar Gooding, Cuba Gooding's brother who was an actor, mostly known for his role in the television show, Smart Guy, with Jason Weaver.

Omar came by to kick it while we were working as well. It was good to see Focus and especially good to work on some music. He told me that he had been letting Dre hear some of the music that we did and was also very happy that I was on the road performing with Brat. To know that Dr. Dre had been exposed to hearing some of my music was insane, but at this point,

MISTER

I'd been around enough to know that there's no need to get too excited, just keep working and see what happens. Either way, I was glad that we were able to connect and the fact we were all the way out in LA was even better. It felt good that he still supported me in everything that I was doing.

Things were going well. I had solid connections, I was traveling, performing on television, and pretty much living the lifestyle of a rap star while out on the road. To top it off, I had just finished working with a producer from Aftermath Records, and wrote a song to be submitted for one of the most anticipated albums. One would say that I was doing pretty damn well. Even still, it hadn't completely registered how far I'd come. It had been a great time out in LA, but now it was time to head out for the first show of the tour in San Jose, headlined by 50 Cent.

Me and Mariah Carey

In the Hollywood Hills, LA

Michael Jackson Star of Fame

Hey

I had to catch the flight from LA to San Jose alone, being that Brat and Uncle Mike were traveling separately, after spending time with family. When I arrived at the hotel, just about all of the artists who were slated to perform were all arriving around the same time. There was an extensive lineup of artists that were performing, but the main acts were Naughty By Nature, Trina, Fabolous, Da Brat, with 50 Cent as the headliner.

It was 2003 and anybody who was into the hip hop culture, knows that 50 Cent's album "Get Rich Or Die Tryin" was the hottest product out, with 50 Cent being the top rap artist in the game. The arena was huge and seated over 20,000-30,000 people!

We did a sound check prior to the show, which was an opportunity to get a feel for the microphone and speaker acoustics. The stage was huge, with lots of room to move around, which meant more work in staying active and to keep moving. I stood at the center of the stage and looked out into this huge empty arena. I couldn't believe that my journey had brought me this far. To think, this place would be packed with people from the front to the back. I instantly got nervous, however, being that we rehearsed thoroughly for this show, I was very prepared to fulfill my hype man duties.

Back at the hotel, we ate and relaxed for a bit, before heading out to the venue for the show that evening. Once we got there, we were led to our dressing room, which was loaded with all the things that Brat had on her rider. A rider is a list of items that all artists request to have in their guest rooms. We had a plethora of food items, along with every kind of alcohol, juices, and water.

A few doors down from our dressing room was 50 Cent's area. He had about five giant sized men, who look like human transformers standing outside of the room. If that wasn't enough, there was about 20-30 street dudes, all with bulletproof vests on. In my mind, I'm thinking this is crazy! Given all of the drama surrounding him at the time, I totally got it.

There was a monitor in the dressing room that allowed us to watch the show that was happening out in the venue. With every rumble from the bass of the music playing and the crowd cheers, I got more and more nervous. The biggest stage that I performed on, was for the Wutang Clan show we did at Earthlink Live in Atlanta. It seated about 2,000 people and that was a large crowd to me. This audience was ten times the size of that and we were all the way on the opposite side of the map.

All types of questions and thoughts were running thru my mind and I officially had to use the bathroom. At this point, I was super nervous and I was trying hard to not let it show. Brat was in her zone and ready for ShowTime. Uncle Mike was also calm and laughing. This was the norm for them, but for me, I was internally freaking out. I decided to step out of the room and walk down the hallway to really, just get away.

While I was out there, I proceeded to head side stage to get a glimpse of Naughty By Nature, who was doing their thing and killing the crowd with back-to-back hits. They had the ultimate show and one of the best I've ever seen to this day! At one point, the lead emcee of the group, Treach, who was shirtless, called the crowd's attention to the tattoo on his arm of the late, great Tupac Shakur. He told the audience that his homie had something to say, so he pointed the mic toward his arm, where the tattoo was, and on cue, "Makaveli in this….!" The voice of Tupac came thru the speakers and the entire crowd lost control, singing every lyric to the hit "Hail Mary" word for word. It was one of the most amazing things I had seen live.

After witnessing that, I went back to the room because it was just about time for us to go up. We did a huddle prayer and headed out towards the main stage. It was the longest walk ever, all the way down the hallway, around the back of the stage, to the other side where we would wait before being announced to go on stage.

Now from this point of view, from behind the tower of speakers, I could see the left side of the venue, from the floor all the way up to the nosebleed sections. The host of the event was on the stage doing a little bit of crowd participation to get them ready for the next act, which was us.

My stomach is turning. There is no bathroom to run to, it's too late. I'm pacing back and forth, holding farts in, because God forbid, I ruin my underwear at a time like this. The hairs on my arm are at attention, with chill bumps all over. I'm handed a cordless microphone and my anxiety goes into overdrive. My eyes started to water. I can feel my heart racing. I feel a panic attack coming. Now, I'm scared and not exactly sure that I'm doing a good job of hiding it. I'm feeling very alone.

I equate this to a feeling I had, as a kid, when I did the daring act of climbing the ladder all the way to the top of a diving board, at the pool. Once I got up there and walked out onto the plank, saw how much of a drop it really was, I was shook, but couldn't turn back or show fear with so many other kids looking on, you gotta Jump.

Inside, I wanted to just scream and cry, to the point, where for almost a split second, I thought of saying, "I can't do this." I think the issue is, I didn't have a buildup to prepare for this. Sure, I had performed a lot of times, in different environments and for a variety of people, from dangerous hoods, to raucous open mic venues, to churches, schools, and theaters. However, the jump in the size of the crowd, was a big one.

The lineup of artists that also were performing were of the elite. I'm going on stage with one of the elite and top legends in the history of hip hop. I don't want to mess up and ruin my opportunity. I talked all this hype of wanting to make it to the Inside, here it is, right here, right now, and what am I doing in the moment? Shook.

I needed to calm my spirit down. All of the weed and alcohol in my system, was not doing the trick. What else could I do? It's literally minutes before we hit that stage. The crowd is so loud that the screams and cheers give off the sound of a distant blend of "hahhhhh." In the midst of all that, I pulled the cell phone out of my pocket and called my mother. She answered, thank God!

I remember her asking me where I was. I had kept her informed everywhere I was going, each time I boarded a plane, so she was aware I was on the tour. I told her that at this present moment, I'm on the side of the stage, about to go on and…just came out with it, "Mom, I'm scared…can you please pray for me?"

MISTER

Without a second to waste, my mom goes "Father, in the name of Jesus…" I pressed the phone into my ear and used the other hand that was holding the cordless, to plug my other ear. I tuned out everything that was going on around me, while my mother prayed for me on the phone. The way the prayer started, ended the same way, "…in Jesus name, Amen." I thanked my mom and she encouraged me to do what I was born to do and that she loved me. We ended the call just in time to hear the host announce us as the next act. "Yall make some noise for Da Braaattt!" Everything slows down and goes silent for me. I can feel my heart pounding and can hear myself breathing. I take a deep inhale, while I make my way up the steps. This is It!

We headed up the stairs onto the stage and went directly into our set. Looking out from the stage, I saw nothing but a sea of people, as far as my eyes could see. As soon as I said "Yo" in the mic, all fear had left the building. I was hype, energized, confident, empowered, and felt like I had arrived!

Uncle Mike rocked out on stage with us as well. Everything we rehearsed went just as planned. We had the crowd rocking out of control with all of the hits Brat kept coming with, from "No One Else featuring Total", "Give It to You", "That's What I'm Looking Fo", "What You Like with Tyrese", leading up to her biggest hit single of "Funkdafied".

We blazed thru the show and I got lost in the moment. This was until, finally, my moment of the show had arrived. Brat stopped the performance to talk to the crowd for a second. She then introduced me, as her new artist, named Mister. She told the crowd to say, "Hey Mister" and an entire crowd of thousands yelled out "Hey Mister". Brat said, "I'm going to have him drop a freestyle for yall." The crowd cheered in anticipation.

As I stood there, with mic in hand, I thought of how everything that I had worked so hard for brought me to this moment. Look at me, I'm just a country kid from Polk County, Florida, with big dreams of being somebody in the world. I wanted to be the President of the United States back then. My travels as a military brat, broadened my scope of the world, and somehow led me to Virginia, where my passion of pursuing this rap thing was honed.

I used to rap at the playgrounds, on the school bus, at the lunch tables, telling anybody who would listen that I was going to make it to the stage. I got a lot of laughs and doubt from my own family even, with numerous setbacks, but here I am. My thoughts go back to Mad Skillz, handing me that microphone for the first time, rhyming on that chair in Richmond, to staring at A Tribe Called Quest through that glass in Norfolk, my first show in Tampa, all the rhyme ciphers at FAMU, the rap battles, to all of the supporters and believers, like Griff, from the Red Train. He believed in me. Focus believed in me. Da Brat saw something in me, enough to give me this opportunity. My family finally came around to believe and support, along with a strong circle of friends.

I do this for them, I do this for my daughter, Genesis Lyric. I want to be an example of **persistence** and perseverance. Sure, I'd dealt with a lot of highs and lows, with plenty of **heartbreaks**, but *this* was my moment of **triumph**. You really can do anything you put your mind to. Just put your mind on the right thing, focus, and let nothing get in your way.

Most importantly, I do this for ME. Have you any idea of what I went thru to get here? After reading this, you certainly do! You know the joys, the pains, the setbacks, and the comebacks. You've taken this journey with me, so I ask you now to stay with me. I'm about to show the world my God-given talent, starting with this crowd, here in San Jose. I made it, finally, I'm on the **Inside!** Oh, what a feeling!

I step forward, "A Yo!"

Feel I was put here to Motivate
Plant seeds let em Cultivate
Spit that pollen
make the whole state of Georgia hate
And like the South, I got sumthin to say
Outkasted coming out of VA
Jersey on, but I ain't coming to play
Stay hungry, too humble at times get in the way
Led astray from whats morally ethic
For more acceptance
Cut up crack pieces when it got hectic
Things I regretted
Stresses of a Dreamchaser
The Meek supposed to Inherit
Back to back losses often I've dealt with
The devil a mess, tugging my Flesh
Pray that God would Just Do It
Put him in Check
I'm one of the best, gunning the rest
Yelling 7th Day on every stage
I ever stepped on
Just pillow talk for those that slept on him
But now erbody woke
Clap for him
Platform
Gorrilla Gang

-   "Good Things", MR Ripley aka M I S T E R

The view of the crowd from the stage…San Jose, w/50 Cent

Pic taken of me and Da Brat on same stage, first show together.

MISTER

MR.

-

In Memory of:

My daddy Kenny, Uncle Tim, my cousin Alysia, cousin Kendrya, Mymease, my Grandmothers Cat, Ola Mae, Lillian, Grandfathers Roosevelt, JB Miller, D.P., James, auntie Laura, auntie Cookie, Uncle Bo, Uncle Sammy, uncle David, uncle Bad Boy, aunt Beulah, friends Roger McBride, Junior, Jamaal Rose, Mel Brikz, and Quan

...May God rest your souls, till we meet again

MISTER

About the Author

Mister Overstreet, commonly referred to as "Mister", currently resides in Atlanta, Ga, with his wife and family. This author is passionate about his music. His recordings can be found on every streaming platform. He has performed on some of the largest stages in the world. He is an established writer, songwriter, videographer, photographer, and video editor, working with the likes of Da Brat, 2 Chainz, Lil Wayne, and many more. Passionate about serving others, with a talent for networking, he is helping other creatives realize their dreams, through his brand, Ishotcha Media.

<u>STAY TUNED FOR MORE IN THE BOOK SERIES, AVAILABLE SOON</u>

*Inside Looking In: Humble Beginnings
*Inside Looking In: Already Famous

*B.O.S.S. – A Curriculum for Aspiring Entrepreneurs
- Business Of Service and Solutions

Visit www.mynamemister.com for more info
IG: @mynamemister
TW: @mynamemister
FB: @mynamemister101